Lost Herself

shell.chelle

Lost Herself
shell.chelle

Copyright © 2024 shell.chelle
Lost Herself

ISBN: 979-8-9912545-0-2

All rights reserved, no part of this publication may be reproduced, distributed, or transmitted by any means without the prior written permission of the author.

Book & Cover Design: Integrative Ink
www.integrativeink.com

Poetry about a girl.
Just a girl,
Living her life.
Writing down her dreams.
Just a girl.
Imperfect and flawed.
Found her love,
Inside of herself.
Writing some words.
Words that became poetry.

These words became a story.
Her Story.
A story of a girl who:

Lost Herself

Found Herself

Then learned to...

Love Herself

This little side note:

This is her experience.
Her point of view.
Her feelings.
Her perspective.
Her story of letting go.
Her story of leaving,
A world of black and white.
Leaving the darkness,
And finding her light.
Her story of arriving,
To where the grey area resides.
This place of surrender.
This place of light.
A story of her memory.
A story of her truth.
A story from her eyes.
A story from her heart.
A story from her mind.
A story that she remembers,
As she listened to herself.
As she listened on her path.
Her path to self-love.
Her path to self-worth.
Her path to authenticity.
Her path to alignment.
Her path to her soul.
Her path.
Her love.
This is her story.

Also, this.
(In very fine print.)

These words.
These are just words.
Words of poetry.
Poetry to read.
These are just words.
Beautiful words.
Words of poetry.

Lost Herself

Lost Herself

She lost herself.
Herself, as she knew her.
She lost herself.
The self she had built.
She lost herself,
Or so she thought.
This was actually the path,
To find her true self.
She had to lose herself,
In order to find.
In order to find her true, authentic self.
She lost herself,
The self that she was.
Her old self...
This was not who she was.
This was not her.
This was her,
Covered in pain.
Herself,
Who she knew.
Herself,
That she showed.
Showed to the world.
This was her mask.
This was her façade.
Putting her mask on,
In order to survive.
Survive in the world,
Where she did not belong.
She did not belong.

Belong in this world.
This world of façades.
This world with masks.
This world of unawareness.
This world of ego.
This world,
Where no one knew their trauma.
This world,
Where everyone wore their masks.
She did not belong here.
She belonged to herself.
Herself that she needed to go out and find.
Underneath this façade.
Herself,
Her soul...
Was buried.
Buried underneath all this pain.
Underneath her trauma.
Her trauma...
She needed to figure this out.
She needed to feel her pain.
Uncover these layers.
Peel back each layer.
Pick up each piece.
Each piece of pain.
Layer by layer.
Until she found herself.
Her true, authentic self.
She kept on digging.
Digging and digging.
Feeling and feeling.

Letting it all go...
She kept going until she found her soul.

She Discovered Herself

This girl.
Oh,
So in love.
In love with her childhood sweetheart.
Her childhood sweetheart,
Stole her heart.
He took her in.
He believed in her.
Took care of her hard,
Without caring for himself.
They didn't know themselves,
Well enough.
To know what they needed,
When times got tough.
Oh,
But they loved.
They were in love.
Until the day,
Where they were both empty.
Empty inside.
Inside of themselves.
Running from themselves.
Choosing a way to soothe their pain.
They both ran away.
Ran away from their love.
Their love for themselves,
As well as their love for each other.
Different worlds,
They were living in.
She became codependent.

He became addicted.
He chose another world,
To help him numb.
She was doing the same,
Just in a much different way.
Trying to save him,
Without caring for herself.
Putting herself aside,
For everyone else.
Different worlds,
They were living in.
They both needed to discover themselves.
They both needed to find out who they truly were.
This broke her,
Watching him.
Watching him,
Deteriorate.
This scared her,
Watching him.
Watching him as he changed.
Changed into someone she didn't know.
She didn't know this guy,
Not anymore.
He told her lies.
So many lies.
He had another life,
On the side.
He was choosing himself,
Over her.
She didn't feel protected,
Not anymore.
He was her safety.

He was her person.
He was her first love.
This broke her heart.
Her heart was shattered.
She had never felt like this before.
She shut herself off.
She hid from the world.
She needed to figure herself out.
She needed to put herself back together again.
She needed to repair,
This damage, that was done.
She needed to repair,
What she was running from.
What was she running from?
What was there?
What was inside of her,
That she needed to repair?
Her childhood self.
Her little girl.
Her little girl,
That she never saw.
Her little girl,
That she never heard.
Her little girl,
That she had dismissed.
Saying goodbye.
Goodbye to him.
Gave her the chance,
To find her inner world.
Her inner girl,
Was there waiting.
Waiting for her.

Waiting all this time.
She had been waiting.
Waiting to be heard.
Waiting to be seen.
Waiting to be understood.
She needed to become whole.
Become whole for herself.
She needed to take her inner girl,
Into her arms.
She found love.
Both for her inner girl and for herself.
She discovered self-love.
She discovered herself.

My Demise

You, disappearing in front of my eyes.
That broke me.
That was my demise.
Our life.
Gone.
Thrown away.
You turned into a person,
I no longer knew.
I didn't know how to deal.
I needed to figure it all out.
On my own.
I closed my heart.
I had no idea,
What that did to me.
Until I took the time,
To go inside.
Inside of myself.
Inward into my heart.
Repair and mend,
My wounds I had.
I couldn't see my wounds,
Because I had you.
We had our life,
Until it disappeared.
I was keeping us afloat,
Keeping your secrets.
Trying to maintain an image,
That was no longer there.
Putting on a façade,
Because I didn't feel safe.

Appearing fake,
Protecting my emotions.
Who could I trust?
If I couldn't even trust you?
I didn't know myself.
Me without you.
Trying to help you,
While I put myself aside.
Trying to keep it together,
Until I no longer could.
I could no longer do it,
Not anymore.
I shut everything down.
I could not put into words.
Not until now.
I had no idea how to even explain.
Explain the feelings that were coming up.
It was all so overwhelming.
I shut everyone out.
No one would know how badly I was hurt.
No one would see my emotions come out.
How could I let anyone close?
Close to me again,
After all of this.
My one true love.
Disappeared.
Betrayal.
I no longer felt safe.
Closed off and shutdown.
I was so badly hurt.
No one would see this.
I would keep it to myself.

I needed to process.
And find out who I am.
Who am I without you?
Who am I,
Just me?
So much to process.
So much to see.
So much to understand.
So much to undo.
So much to feel.
I needed to give back to myself.
I really needed to recover and heal.
See through a lens.
A lens without you.
This lens I looked through,
For so many years.
This lens was fogged.
This lens was not clear.
This lens I looked through,
Was covered in fog.
Fogged with childhood trauma and beliefs.
Limiting beliefs.
Beliefs that weren't true.
Fogged with you.
Fogged with our life.
I needed to clear this lens clean.
I needed to look through a clear lens.
A lens that I could see through.
I needed to believe and trust in myself.
Build a life I always dreamed of.
Let go of this lens.
Let go of you.

Let go of us.
Let go of that life.
I am finally grateful.
Grateful for my demise.

Closure

I had to find,
The end all by myself.
I had to find,
My own closure.
I couldn't ask you questions.
Because you told me so many lies.
I couldn't share my feelings,
Because you weren't present to hear them.
You made me believe what you wanted me to believe.
You painted a picture of yourself,
To me.
You had another life,
That you kept from me.
There were so many stories.
So many lies.
So much stolen.
So much betrayal.
I was barely breathing.
I was barely living.
I was barely keeping myself afloat.
I was in survival mode.
I kept going and going,
Because that's all I could do.
I couldn't lean on you.
This was all new.
Your behavior,
Your voice,
You no longer told the truth.
There were even times you threw me down.
You put your hands on me.

And told me,
Not to make a sound.
This didn't happen a lot...
But the times that it did,
Were engrained in my mind.
You told me not to tell anyone,
To protect yourself.
That was all you cared about.
You. You. You.
That is all you could see.
You no longer protected me.
You were not my provider.
You no longer lifted me up.
You stopped making me laugh.
Now, all I was,
Was scared.
You became sneaky.
You became mean.
All you would do now is steal from me.
This became my normal,
I was all alone.
I went for help once,
And once again,
I was betrayed.
This made me stay silent.
My life no longer had vibrance.
You watched me struggle,
You watched me cry.
You watched as I crumbled.
I knew that my life with you,
Could not continue.
I looked at you,

With fear in my eyes.
And couldn't trust you.
Trust you at all.
I needed to leave.
I needed to breathe.
I just wanted out.
I did this all,
By myself.
I had to go,
I had to leave,
Without any closure.
I couldn't talk anything through,
With you...
Because nothing ever made any sense.
There were threats,
Followed with lies,
And deceit from you.
And I never knew,
If I was safe.
I became cold.
I closed my heart.
That is not a way to live,
This is not what I signed up for.
I left without a proper goodbye.
Because I knew,
You could not give me that.
You stopped giving,
A long time ago.
All of your actions,
Became unforgiving.
All you would do now,
Is take from me.

You took everything.
You took yourself.
You took our life.
You took my heart.
You took your soul.
You took my closure.
I couldn't go to you for anything,
I lost all trust.
You used to make me feel safe.
And all I am now,
Is afraid.
Looking back,
At this big picture...
I sit in disbelief.
How did this happen?
This person I knew,
Turned into someone I didn't know.
This was the hardest part,
For me to see.
I couldn't understand.
Where did you go?
I had no closure.
Closure,
From you.
I had to do it...
All alone.

The Time It Was Finalized

There were phone calls,
And emails.
There were conversations,
And texts.
I don't remember,
Any of it.
I blocked it all out.
Because the pain was so intense.
There was so much sadness.
Until one day,
It all came back.
Flashback by flashback,
I started to remember.
The end was here,
The papers were drawn up.
I remember signing and just feeling numb.
I signed my name to the paper.
I walked out of the office,
And didn't look back.
I knew this is what was needed to be done.
But I didn't know,
What would follow.
I signed my name on that paper,
Not knowing how I would feel much later.
That day was the day,
It became finalized.
The day that said,
Our marriage was done.
The day that ended,
All of our love.

I signed my name,
Like it was nothing.
I closed the door,
Expecting to feel something.
It didn't come that day,
Or even in weeks.
I shoved it all down,
Because that's all I could do.
Because I didn't want to face you.
Your love for me,
My love for you.
And how we lived so happily.
That was a time,
I never wanted to forget.
I kept all of those memories so close to my heart.
And even on that day,
That I signed our marriage away.
I kept the good times,
So deep inside.
I never wanted the end,
To be finalized.
How could this happen?
How could this be?
That our love was over,
You were my family.
How do I say goodbye to this?
Our love was all I knew.
You were the only one,
I ever committed to.
I told you vows,
That I wanted to keep.
I gave you my heart,

For you to hold deep.
Deep in your heart.
And deep in your soul.
That is where,
I believed I would stay.
I never thought,
That you would leave.
I never thought,
That you would change.
Change into someone,
That I was afraid of.
Change into someone,
I wouldn't know.
Change into someone,
I didn't recognize.
When you changed and started a life,
That I didn't fit into.
When you started making choices,
That I couldn't understand.
That was a journey,
Towards the end.
Towards the end of You & I.
The end of something,
That I didn't know how to feel.
The end of something,
That I tried to fix so many times.
The end of something,
I couldn't even begin to process.
The end of our marriage,
Was the end of so much more to come.
The end of our marriage,
Awakened my soul.

That signature on those papers,
Signified a new journey...
That was out of my control.
The signature that was signed,
Was a new start.
The signature that was signed,
Is when I closed my heart.
This was the time,
It was finalized.
This was the time,
That my old life would meet,
The beginning of my new life.
On this journey,
I would say goodbye.
I would have to part ways,
With all that I knew.
And that all started,
With saying goodbye to you.
I wasn't ready.
I didn't know how.
This was not what I planned.
I planned to love you until forever.
I planned to be by your side,
And leave you never.
Signing my name on this document,
Was something that came so fast.
I knew I needed to do this,
Because I no longer felt safe.
Safe with you around.
Safe in your arms.
It was my way out of this darkness.
That I never wanted to be in.

I wanted a life filled with joy.
With you by my side.
Now I understand,
That neither of us was ready.
Ready for what life would bring along.
We both needed tools.
That we didn't have.
Tools that we needed,
To make ourselves strong.
Now I understand,
That the day our end was finalized.
Was the day,
I would be given tools and lessons.
I needed these tools,
Before I could feel the pain.
The pain.
Of saying goodbye to you.
You are in my heart,
You are a distant memory now.
I will never stop caring,
But I had to let go.
I had to let go of our love.
This love was weighing me down.
This pain I shoved away,
Finally made its way up,
And now I am in agony.
This love was so sacred.
This love was so pure.
It all ended,
With a signature.
I signed my name,
On that paper.

But you still lived on,
Inside of me.
I didn't want to believe,
That you chose to become,
Something that I didn't know.
I see you now,
And I realize...
That I was not living in reality.
The reality is that you became someone else.
Someone that chose darkness over light.
Someone that was destroyed,
By another life.
That life could not be mine,
I had to go a different way.
Which is why,
I finalized.
I finalized the ending,
But I still could not see.
I could not see,
All the hurt that was inside of me.
I held on so tight.
Even after,
All the signatures were done.
And the papers were filed.
I was holding on.
In my dreams,
I could still see your smile.
My dreams would elaborate...
A life that could never be,
With you and me.
You were not the same,
And neither was I.

So why hold on?
Feel this pain.
This pain made its way up in waves.
I am close to the end,
Of feeling this agony.
I realize now that when I give my love,
I love hard and really deep.
I have learned that letting go,
Is a part of life.
Life is change.
Constant change and nothing ever stays the same.
And now I know,
As I move on...
Not to hold on.
Hold on,
So tight.
I can be free now.
Free from your love.
Free from what we had.
But I will never forget our memories.
I will never forget the person you were,
And the heart that lives inside of you.
No matter the darkness,
That you are in,
Your heart is still there.
The beauty is there.
That is what you gave and showed to me.
No matter what I went through,
As bad as it was...
I will always know that beautiful heart,
Is inside of you.
That was all before.

That was the old you.
I have found acceptance.
I can finally see clear.
That signature I signed,
Was not for an ending.
It was not about,
You and me.
That signature I signed,
It was for my destiny.
That signature I signed,
It was all for my freedom.

You Were My Person

You treated me like gold.
You made me your world.
You were so good to me.
You would have done anything for me.
You gave me your all.
You gave me direction.
You supported me always.
You were always there,
Until you weren't.
Until you left.
Until you changed.
Until you lied.
Until you deceived.
Do you have any idea what that did to me?
Do you have any idea what that felt like?
My one person.
My one and only.
I know I wasn't perfect,
But I loved you.
I never had eyes for anyone else.
My eyes were on you.
My eyes were for you.
My heart was given.
Given to you,
Without question.
Without hesitation.
I was never guarded.
Guarded with you.
I trusted you fully.
You were my person.

Until you weren't.
Do you have any idea what that did to me?
Your lies.
Your life,
Separate from mine.
Separate from ours.
You became distant.
You became different.
Lie after lie.
Betrayal after betrayal.
My safety shattered.
My trust taken.
Taken away.
Taken by you.
My heart was broken.
It was completely shattered.
My heart,
In pieces.
So many tears.
So much sadness.
I had no idea what to do.
I had no idea how to get through it.
I had no idea who I was.
I didn't have the tools,
To handle this.
I didn't even know.
Know what to do.
I couldn't feel.
I had to shut it off.
I became numb.
I became distant too.
Run away.

Run away from it at all.
Run far from these feelings.
These feelings I shoved away.
Run far away from the pain I felt.
Any sort of pain,
I pushed it away.
Put a smile on my face,
Because I couldn't imagine trusting.
Trusting people with this pain.
I didn't know who to trust if I couldn't trust you.
How do I admit?
Admit that I am falling apart?
Admit my pain.
Admit my hurt.
How do I admit it?
When I didn't have trust.
I didn't have trust in anyone else.
You were my person,
Until you weren't.
My trust was in you,
Until you took it.
You took it for you,
And left me empty.

I Needed...

When I lost our love,
I lost myself.
When I said goodbye to you,
I had to say goodbye to myself.
To the part of me,
That had love for you.
I had to mourn our love.
I had to mourn you.
I had to mourn myself,
And my life with you.
I will never return,
To that girl.
To that girl,
That everyone knew.
When I lost our love,
I lost myself.
Who was I now?
Who do I want to be?
What do I want now,
That it is just me?
I needed to search.
Search for my soul.
I needed to find my true self.
I needed to leave behind,
All that I knew.
I needed to allow myself to grieve.
I needed to learn to nurture me.
I needed to put myself first.
I needed rest.
I needed to understand.

Understand that you had your own path.
Understand that your path,
Had nothing to do with me.
Understand that my path was waiting for me.
I needed to forgive you.
I needed to let you go.
I needed to be ready.
Ready for this step.
I needed to bring myself back up.
I needed to come up,
From being down.
I needed to figure out,
What I wanted.
I needed to figure myself out.
Me, myself & I.
I needed to allow myself to feel.
I found myself,
Through the pain.
I found myself,
When I let everything go.
I found myself.
She was always there.
She has been inside,
All along.

My Old Life

I can't believe I lived that life.
I can't believe the way I was treated.
I can't believe how you talked to me.
I can't believe how you manipulated me.
I can't believe how you yelled at me.
I can't believe how you changed.
I can't believe how you hurt my heart.
I can't believe that I had to find a new start.
A new start without you.
A new start without your lies.
A new start without your chaos.
A new start without your betrayal.
A new start without anxiety.
Anxiety was what I felt,
When you were near.
Anxiety was what I felt,
Because I didn't feel safe.
I used to have panic attacks,
And thought they were normal.
I accepted them,
To be part of my life.
I accepted that my life would be this way.
The way it was at the end.
I was so beaten down.
I was so destroyed.
I was so deeply saddened.
I was so exhausted.
It is not until now,
That I look back.
I look back on that life,

In disbelief.
I look back on that life,
With tears in my eyes.
I look back on that life,
With disappointment.
I look back on that life,
With embarrassment.
Embarrassment that I put up with all that.
Embarrassment that I had just accepted.
Accepted that my life was this way.
I felt shame that my life was this way.
I felt shame that the person I chose,
Did not keep me safe.
He left me for drugs, at the end of the day.
He left me for people,
People that made me feel unsafe.
He brought these people into my safe space.
He brought these people around for him.
To benefit his needs.
To benefit his life.
These people were unsafe.
They were unsafe for me.
How could this person that I loved so much,
Betray me this way?
Throw our life that we had made,
Completely away.
Throw it all away.
Our life is gone.
You chose another one.
A life of darkness.
You chose addiction.
You chose a madness,

That will never bring peace.
You chose a chaos,
Over me.
This saddens my soul.
This saddens my heart.
I am feeling this now.
This feeling burns.
This ache that I have,
It is a grief.
This grief has come over me.
This grief is a drain.
A drain over me.
I have pushed it away,
So many times.
I didn't know that I had it in me.
Had it in me,
To sit and feel this.
This wave flowing through me.
It is so large.
Probably the largest,
That I have felt.
This life we made.
Our life together.
This destructive chaos,
That I knew.
This betrayal is something I should never know.
Not from someone,
That I had in my heart.
This betrayal destroyed me.
This pain brought me down.
This pain created a wound in me.
A wound in me,

That I would have to feel.
Caring for you,
Ruined me.
Caring for a person,
Who was slowly killing me.
Killing my soul,
And burning my love.
My old life,
Was fire.
My old life,
Was toxic.
Toxic for my soul.
My old life,
Shattered my heart.
My old life,
Kicked me down.
Kicked me down,
To my lowest.
The lowest I have ever felt.
My old life,
Wasn't me.
It was not who I am.
I had to bury her,
Underneath the chaos.
I buried her for you.
I chose you,
Over me.
I chose others,
Over myself.
I buried the real me.
She was covered,
With so much pain.

I have uncovered her now.
This blazing fire,
I have put out.
I'm putting it out now.
Once and for all.
Feel this grief.
Feel it all.
My final grief.
Grief for you.
Grief for our life.
My old life.
My old self.
Grieving the betrayal and abandonment.
Grieving the mess.
Grieving the heartache.
Grieving the chaos.
Grieving my old life.
A final goodbye.
A final grief.

You Are Not Alone

I watched you go down a hole.
I watched you avoid.
I watched you leave,
A world behind.
All because you just couldn't see.
You couldn't find a way to cope.
And you are not alone.
There are too many that this happens to.
There are so many lives lost,
To this deep destructive way.
So many loved ones,
Taken away.
It is the hardest thing to watch.
When a person you love,
With your whole heart isn't really there.
I can't even explain in words,
What it was like watching that.
It is something I never want to see again,
Which is why I had to go.
It was the hardest thing I ever did,
Was watch you go down that hole.
So many go through this,
You are not alone.
I always wanted you to know,
That you weren't the only one.
I sacrificed myself for you,
For far too long.
All I ever wanted was for you,
To see what I saw.
This path was not right for you,

But you were choosing it anyway.
This path is what sucks our loved ones away.
This path,
Takes your smile.
It takes away the joy.
It takes away your spark.
It took everything away.
Don't you want those things back?
Why can't you see?
I will never stop,
Having hope for you.
I will pray every day,
That one day you will decide.
That you will choose you.
And I hope that you don't ever feel,
Like you are all alone.
You are never alone,
There is always help.
You will know what to do.
Everyone needs,
Something to cope.
Everyone needs,
Something to soothe.
It never had to be drugs,
Why did it have to be that?
The choices we make,
Aren't always right.
Sometimes we fail.
Failing is okay.
If we get back up,
Always start again.
That is what matters.

Take that pressure off.
There is no perfection.
There is no right way.
Sometimes it takes,
A whole bunch of times to find ourselves.
To find what is right.
To find our path.
To find our way.
You chose this,
And I chose that.
And neither one is wrong.
But it is one that lifts,
And one that destroys,
And we must make the choice.
We must find what works for us.
It is all inside.
Everything that we need,
It is within.
It is how we find it,
It is always there.
Life is hard,
Life is constant,
And we must cope through.
There is suffering.
There is loss.
There is hardship and pain.
We must find a way,
Through the discomfort.
We must find our way.
We must find our path.
Finding a way to soothe ourselves,
Without dimming our own light.

I watched you go down a hole,
That was so dark and cold.
I couldn't go there with you,
I had a different path.
I had to find a way to cope,
When you chose a life of drugs.
You found a way to cope,
Deep down in that hole.
That was you,
And this was me,
Watching you disappear.
I still have hope,
For you every day.
That you find your joy.
I pray to God,
That you have found other ways.
Other ways to cope.
I pray that you get out,
Of that deep darkness that you were in.
And I pray that you,
Find your light...
That was there all along.
I held on to your light.
The light that I saw in you.
This beautiful you.
Your beautiful heart.
I pray that your journey,
Will be filled with so much light.
I pray that you are guided,
To give up your old ways.
I pray that you choose your goodness.
Choose that... over the darkness.

But all of that is in your hands.
And I will surrender to that.
I had to begin to believe,
That your faith was out of my control.
I will pray for you.
Take it day by day.
Each day is a new chance,
To begin again and choose.
Choose to begin,
Each new day.
And put down your old ways.
I still find it very hard,
To picture you that way.
The last time I saw you,
That was one of my hardest days.
I still see your eyes,
Looking at me.
You didn't say a word.
I turned away,
Without saying goodbye.
Not because I didn't care.
I cared too much,
And I couldn't breathe.
I couldn't watch you that way.
It was breaking my heart.
It was breaking my soul.
I had nothing left.
The you that I hold in my heart,
Was the you, before that hole.
It was the you, filled with joy,
That gave me so much love.
This is who I decide to see.

And that is who I hope,
That you, one day, choose to be.
It is a new day,
To see in yourself.
That there is so much beauty in that heart of yours.
Every day, I send you love.
And hope that you understand.
Understand that each new day that starts,
Is a day that you can choose to begin.
Start over again.
Start again.
Each new day is a new day,
And it is never too late.
A whole new journey that waits for you.
One that is filled with light and peace.
It is never too late to begin again.
It will be a whole new start.
Once you find you,
The darkness will start to fade.
And you will start to see,
That you were always there.
You were there all along,
You just couldn't see.

This Pain

How could you?
How could you cause me so much pain?
How can I love ever again?
How can I trust anyone again?
My heart.
This pain.
I loved you so much.
I loved you with everything.
Everything I had.
And now.
Now I can't imagine loving again.
I can't open my heart.
I can't let anyone in.
My heart.
My cries.
My tears.
My love for you,
Was given from my heart.
Straight from my heart.
Your place was there.
I had no idea what would come.
Come while letting go of you.
I had no idea,
This pain.
This pain I will have to feel to love again.
Lose you,
To love again.
Will I be able to?
I owe myself this.
I owe myself,

To give you up.
I owe myself,
To let you go.
I owe myself this.
I owe myself love.
I owe myself to let go.
I owe myself to move on.
I owe myself healing.
I owe myself releasing.
I have repaired my heart,
Without your help.
I have repaired my heart,
By feeling this pain.
This pain that you caused me.
This pain that came,
From loving you.

She Trusted Her Gut

He had a whole other life outside of theirs.
He turned into Dr. Jekyll, Mr. Hyde.
She never knew if he would be home.
She never knew if he would be high.
She feels like she never knew him at all.
She never knew the truth,
But she trusted her gut.
Her gut would tell her everything.
Everything she needed to know.
Nothing made any sense.
Her life had changed.
She became scared.
She kept her mouth shut,
She didn't tell anyone.
She didn't tell anyone what she was experiencing.
She kept every little secret,
To protect him.
Her money was stolen,
She lived with these lies.
He started to bring unsafe people around.
Into their house.
They would come.
He lied about these people.
His crew had changed.
More money gone.
The car was repossessed.
He lied about that too,
He told her some story that "made sense."
Nothing really made any sense,
But she didn't know any other way out.

She was beaten down so much.
Her reality was blurred.
This taught her that she couldn't trust.
Couldn't trust,
Anyone but herself.
She shut down.
She was numb.
All she had,
Was her gut.
Her gut told her every time.
Every time,
He told her a lie.
Every time he wasn't home,
And said he was somewhere else.
Every time there was an elaborate story,
About something gone.
It disappeared.
Nothing disappeared.
It was either stolen or sold.
Sold for cash.
Cash for him.
Cash for his problem.
His problem he never had,
According to him.
She was constantly bailing him out.
She was constantly giving him money.
"I'll pay you back," he said.
Nothing was paid back.
He took and took and took from her.
He took her money,
But he also took her soul.
He took her heart,

He took what was left.
He sucked it all,
Out of her.
Until there was nothing left.
She was just a shell.
A shell of a person.
Hollow inside.
He would blame her.
He would yell for no apparent reason.
This wasn't him.
The him she knew.
He would put her down,
All while she stood by his side.
Stood by his side until the very last chance.
Fighting for him,
She gave him one last chance.
One last chance to get him help.
Get help for himself,
And also for her.
But also, for them.
Save their love.
Save what they built.
Please get clean,
Please do this.
One last chance.
She stood by him until she couldn't.
She could no longer breathe.
She could no longer stand up.
There was nothing left.
She had nothing to give.
She couldn't live like this anymore.
She fell to the ground.

She shut down.
She shut down one final time.
She knew she needed to choose herself.
She knew she needed to follow her gut.
She couldn't do this,
Not anymore.
She finally gave up,
And chose herself.

The Final Pieces

I am finally ready.
Ready to let you go.
Release you.
Release our love.
Release this torture.
This torture inside of me.
I am finally ready to release you for good.
I have been carrying this burden.
This burden of you.
This is a burden.
A burden I carry.
I am finally ready.
Ready to release you.
You took my heart with you.
You took it with you,
When you left.
You tore it out.
Right out of my chest.
You tore it out.
Each time you lied.
You tore it out.
Each time you denied.
Denied your actions.
Denied the truth.
Denied what I saw you do.
Denied my words.
Denied my love.
You tore it out.
Each time you left.
You tore it out.

Each word you said.
You tore it out.
Each time you stole.
You stole from me.
How could you?
Why did you?
I don't understand.
My heart was stomped on,
By this disease.
This disease,
That took my heart from me.
Every word you did not mean.
Every word you told me.
Those words were lies.
To protect yourself.
And every time,
You protected yourself.
Each time,
You tore my heart out.
I still don't know,
What the truth is.
Because you distorted everything you said.
You distorted my beliefs.
You distorted my trust.
You distorted my heart.
You distorted my eyes.
You distorted our love.
You distorted our vows.
You distorted our life,
That we built.
You took my heart,
When you left.

You took my heart,
Each time you promised.
Each time you promised,
It would get better.
Each time you promised,
You would do better.
Each time you promised,
You would not lie again.
Each time you promised,
Yet again.
So many empty promises.
So many empty words.
So many chances I gave you,
To make it right.
You took my heart with you,
Along with my safety.
I put my trust in your hands.
I put my love for you,
In my heart.
And in return,
You shattered my heart.
You broke it into a million pieces.
And left it here.
All the pieces,
For me to pick up.
Piece by piece,
I pick up.
I pick them up.
All the pieces,
For me to mend.
Each piece,
I pick up.

Each piece,
Is pain.
Each piece,
Is agony.
Each piece,
Is torture.
I am finally getting to the final pieces.
These final pieces,
Are the hardest.
These final pieces.
I must have saved.
I must have saved them,
Until I was strong enough to feel them.
I must have saved them,
Because my love for you was so strong.
I must have saved them,
It was my way of holding on.
Holding on to our love.
Holding on to you.
I kept picking them up.
I kept trying to feel them.
I kept shoving them down.
I kept putting this off.
Putting off these final pieces.
I am sick of feeling.
These final pieces.
This final release.
I need to release you.
Release this risk.
The risk I took.
To fall in love.
This risk I took.

I opened my heart.
This risk I took.
The risk of love.
Falling in love,
Is falling into the unknown.
Falling.
Trusting.
Full surrender.
I am releasing all of this.
These final pieces.
I am ready to hold them.
I am ready to feel this agony of you.
This love I had for you,
I am releasing.
I am no longer holding onto you.
I can no longer carry this burden.
This burden of these final pieces.

Years Later

Years later.
I am still dealing with this.
I am still dealing with the day,
You tore my heart out of my chest.
I am laying here,
In this aftermath.
I am still dealing with all these emotions.
Emotions,
I shoved down.
So, I could just be okay.
So, I could just move on.
Build a new life,
And look strong.
That didn't work.
The building a new life,
Without dealing with my stress.
Building a new life comes when you let go.
I was holding on.
Holding on so tight.
I just wanted to be alright.
Strength comes from letting myself feel.
Avoiding and shoving everything away.
Running from my pain.
That is not building strength.
I didn't want to look.
I didn't want to see.
I didn't want to feel reality.
I numbed myself,
I ran away.
And now years later,

Here I am.
Feeling heavy.
These emotions have come up.
I can't push them down,
Not anymore.
I am aware.
Aware of myself.
Aware of this pain.
Aware of these emotions.
My body is telling me.
I am listening.
Here I am,
Years later.
Feeling weighed down.
Feeling betrayed.
How did I end up in this madness?
This madness inside of me?
How did this happen?
I need to let it go.
This will be my intention.
Moving forward.
Please get this out.
Out of me.
I give myself permission.
Permission to feel.
I am sitting in reality,
Without the illusion.
The illusion I built,
For my own safety.
I am removing my armor.
I am removing my shields.
I am safe now.

With each breath in,
I will breathe in peace.
With each exhale,
I will breathe out this chaos.
I will bring healing.
To my body.
To myself.
I will release.
Release the past.
I will release these limiting beliefs.
That have been holding me back.
I will release these emotions,
That keep me weighed down.
I will let myself feel.
Feel this grief.
This grief that comes,
From letting go.
Let everything go.
Everything I know.
Embracing the unknown.
Embracing a life.
A life I waited for.
A life without burden.
My burdens I will drop.
The chaos I knew,
I am walking away.
Years later,
I am free.

She Needed Help

Every time she went for help,
She was shut down.
She went to people that she loved.
She went to people that she trusted.
Basically, her family.
She loved them so much.
She begged and pleaded.
Pleaded for help.
And each time she did,
She was shut down.
She was gas lit.
She was dismissed.
She was humiliated and defeated.
She was minimized and lied to.
Betrayal is what she knew.
She knew it well.
She had tears in her eyes,
As she looked up at the one person she trusted.
She went to him for help.
He told her he would help her.
He listened all week,
She told him everything she knew.
And then he turned on her,
Right in front of her eyes.
He put her down.
He turned on her.
He turned on her,
When she was completely kicked down.
She needed help,
But he didn't care.

He shamed her.
He blamed her,
And made it all about him.
He is the rock star,
And she was nothing.
She had real emotion.
She was on the floor crying.
She needed help so badly.
Her husband just put his hands on her.
Thew her down,
And took away her phone.
"Is she always like this?
No wonder you don't come home."
He said this to her husband,
As she was on the floor.
On the floor,
Helpless.
Because she reached out for help.
He won't be brought down.
Brought down by her.
He is clearly insecure.
Insecure with himself.
He will keep turning on her,
By abusing her.
Manipulative tactics,
Brought her to tears.
This made her feel afraid,
Like she was unsafe.
She wasn't safe,
To go to them for help.
They became defensive,
They made it all about them.

They were in denial,
And she shut down.
She shut down,
And never reached out for help.
She kept everything in.
Everything to herself.
Because each time she needed help,
She was dismissed.

I Understand The Denial

I understand the denial,
Believe me, I do.
I understand that you didn't want to see,
Because that was me too.
I have empathy for you,
I am letting you know.
I was angry with you for a while.
I have anger at times,
For you still.
But I understand the denial.
Believe me, I do.
I was there once.
I stayed there for a while.
I lived with it.
I dealt with it.
I tried to accept it.
The same process as you,
I was there once before.
I understand the denial.
It is part of the process.
I just wish you didn't treat me like shit,
While you were in it.
I have empathy for you.
Believe me, I do.
But I still don't understand why you beat me up now.
Do I intimidate you?
Is that why you trash my name still?
I did nothing to you,
So, I don't understand.
Understand your ill will,

Lost Herself

Towards who I am.
I understand your denial.
Believe me, I do.
I know you care.
I know your heart is there.
I know there is love inside of you.
Is this your defense?
Whatever it is,
I understand your denial.
Believe me, I do.
What I don't understand is you,
Still beating me down.
Years later,
Is your denial still there?
Or you really dislike me that much?
I'm not sure what I did,
Other than ask for your help.
Ask you to leave your denial state.
See what is real,
And do what needs to be done.
I spoke the truth,
And you didn't want to hear.
Someone else's problem doesn't reflect who you are.
Someone else's problem has nothing to do with you.
You care so much about image.
You care about how it looks.
You care about the picture you paint to the world,
Instead of what is real.
What is real?
People are not perfect.
People live with pain.
People sometimes self sooth.

Self sooth in different ways.
They want to numb the pain,
And this has nothing to do with you.
There is no reason to shame.
Shame the people you love.
Shame them for not being perfect,
And not maintaining an image for you.
I understand your denial.
Believe me, I do.
What I don't understand,
Is how you treated me.
You treated me like shit,
And made it all about you.
So concerned with what others would say about you.
Instead of being honest.
Honest with yourself.
Honest with a problem.
A problem that isn't even yours.
Make it go away,
By shoving it under the rug.
What I still don't understand,
Is your lack of accountability.
You throw your insecurities onto everyone else,
So, you don't have to see.
This is why you stay in denial,
And it just seems like you never leave.

Get Over Yourself

Get over yourself.
You really aren't that special.
Get over yourself.
You bring abuse to others.
Get over yourself and the image.
The fake image you paint to the world.
This image isn't even real.
After all these years,
You still haven't learned.
Still acting the same,
Flaunting your money.
Still trashing my name,
When I did nothing but love.
Love you and your kid.
Love you and your family.
You were the one that I went to.
You were the one that I trusted.
You were the one,
That probably could have helped the most.
But you didn't want to look at or see yourself.
You wanted to stay up on that pedestal.
That pedestal.
Your ego.
You wouldn't step out of it.
Get over yourself,
You're not that big of a deal.
Especially with how you treat people,
Behind closed doors.
Someone once told me,
People see who you are.

People see how you carry yourself.
People notice that you are genuine.
That is all you have to do.
Let down the façade.
Get off that pedestal.
Being up there doesn't matter.
Coming off that pedestal,
Will be really hard.
You will see things you don't want to see,
That you have been covering up.
Get over yourself,
Please come down.
Get off that pedestal.
It's not even helpful,
Being up there.
Get over yourself,
That is now who you really are.
It's okay to show your flaws,
And let the fake image fade away.

My Heart.

My heart.
Protected.
By barriers.
And Walls.
And shields.
Blocked off.
I have such a beautiful heart.
My heart is BIG.
I gave it away once.
I loved...
With
Every
Cell
In
My
Body.
I loved...
With my whole heart.
Everyone was let in.
I love you.
With all
Of
My heart
And soul.
That is how,
I handled my heart.
All
Or
Nothing.
I gave,

All of my
Love.
Give and give and give.
Give all of my love.
Until it shattered.
My heart.
It broke,
Into a
Million pieces.
I close it off,
All by myself.
I remember,
Closing it off.
I remember,
Building the walls.
I remember,
Putting up the shields.
Guard it.
Protect it.
Everyone out.
How do I fix it?
Now that it broke?
I have never
Felt this
Before.
I will learn to protect it...
But now it
Is not
Even a whole heart.
Guarded.
Pieces. Shattered. Fragments.
How do I make it whole again?

I will guard my heart.
Repair.
Mend.
Cries.
So many tears.
I can't breathe.
This pain in
My chest.
It hurts.
Will this stop?
Are these
Cries
Repairing it?
Or will it
Stay
Shattered?
Like this?
I've learned to
Pray
Through this process.
While this
Sharp shooting
Pain
Radiates through
My soul.
I will continue to feel,
This darkness.
I will guard,
And protect,
Until I decide.
It is a choice,
I must make.

I built these walls.
It is me,
That will tear them down.
Until these walls
Are down,
I will not feel any pain.
It is in these
Cries,
That I figured it out.
This is me.
Tearing them down.
This is my choice,
Removing the walls.
I will have to commit,
To feel.
And it is then,
That I will heal.
I realize this,
So, I decide...
That it is time,
To work on my walls.
These walls,
Around my heart.
Moments pass by,
That I will never forget.
I will have to see your face.
I will find that,
If I want to repair my heart...
I will have to find forgiveness.
Forgiveness for you.
I will have to see,
And come to terms,

That I handed you over my heart, effortlessly.
It was me who found trust in you.
It was me that chose to live unprotected.
I understand that you took part.
But it was me,
Too,
That gave away my whole heart.
It was me,
That didn't love myself.
I can repair it,
That is my goal.
I will fix it,
So that I can feel,
Love again.
For myself, this time.
I will start with myself.
Going all of these years,
With shields and protection around my love.
I realize now,
That life is not worth living like that.
Life will be suffering,
And life will be joy.
But I won't feel any joy,
If I don't let the light in.
I now have the tools that I need to heal.
I will let love in,
I will face my fear.
Embrace the good,
And feel the light.
I will open my heart,
And
This will be my choice.

It is in the act of surrender,
Where I will find my mended heart.
This is where I meet,
The love of my life.
And it has always been and will always be,
ME.

Survival Mode

My whole life.
Survival mode on.
Running.
From myself.
Running.
From my trauma.
Running.
From my problems.
Running.
From my pain.
I ran.
From my own body.
I ran.
From my own feelings.
I didn't want to deal.
I couldn't deal.
I couldn't face what happened.
What happened to me.
I felt unsafe.
I needed protection.
I learned.
Protection was up to me.
I protect myself.
I needed to learn how.
How to keep myself safe.
What does this look like?
This was up to me.
I learned this,
Finally.
Get myself out.

Out of survival mode.
Out of flight.
Out of fight.
Out of freeze.
Get myself out.
Out of all of these.
Get myself back into my own body.
Return back home.
Back home,
To myself.
Get myself out.
Out of survival mode.

Quiet

Peace.
Solitude.
It is so quiet.
Stillness.
Silence.
Soundless.
No more chaos.
No more noise.
It is just quiet now.
I hear nothing.
I see nothing,
I found this.
I love this.
Tranquility.
It is so calm.
Softness.
And beauty.
So peaceful.
Just be.
That's it.
In this quiet.
Nothing.
Or maybe…
It is everything.
This is everything.
Everything to me.
Safety.
Listen.
There is nothing.
Nothing to hear.

In this Stillness.
Inside of this stillness.
A plain white room.
A big open field.
A calm ocean
Or lake.
Anywhere that is quiet.

Love Of My Life

Everyone talks about the love of their life.
That there is supposed to be that person,
Who is out there, who is your one true love.
Everyone talks about finding that person.
But what if that person is me?
I will become everything that I want.
I will be the love of my life.
I will give myself love,
I will hug myself when I am down.
I will look to myself,
For advice.
I will be there,
At the end of the day.
And after all of this,
I will find...
That I was the one.
I was it.
My own love of my life.
It was me,
All along.
All these stories...
Of going on dates,
Meeting different men.
What is it for?
Why am I doing this?
Looking for intimacy.
Looking for attraction.
Looking for compatibility.
Looking for someone I can trust.
A man of his word.

A man of action.
A man of integrity.
A man of growth.
A man with confidence.
Honesty and loyalty.
Strong and courageous.
Independent and masculine.
Self-awareness and brave.
A reflector with goals.
Respectful and smart.
Funny and committed.
Thoughtful and introspective.
Deep and dedicated.
Open and sensitive.
Spiritual and free.
Vulnerability.
Understanding and empathetic.
Loving and fun.
Awakened and conscious.
A protector.
A nature lover,
And must love dogs.
This criteria,
Is he out there?
Yes, of course.
But first,
I will find,
All of that in myself.
Once I find all of that in myself,
That is who I will attract.
We attract what we are.
So, what I am looking for,

Is what I must become.
Become my person.
My number one.

Grief

Grief.
It comes in waves.
So many waves of discomfort and pain.
Heaviness.
Exhaustion.
Another wave is here.
Sometimes,
It causes me to be glued down to my pillow.
Glued down to my bed.
I can't move.
This wave feels really bad.
It feels so heavy,
At it's peak.
Drowning and crying,
Let me release.
Get this out,
Make room for more.
Another wave,
Will come to explore.
Grief will come,
Whenever it wants.
I let it come,
I let it go.
This wave feels like I am weighed down.
I just want to be alone,
I want no one around.
Sometimes it feels empty.
Sometimes it feels lonely.
Sometimes I am angry.
Sometimes I can't sleep.

Sometimes it's hard to breathe.
Sometimes I feel numb.
My grief makes room,
For many new thoughts.
My grief has changed me,
Through the loss.
I will never again,
Be the same.
I will take each wave,
As it comes.
I will feel this change,
In my body and my brain.
I will accept the pain,
For what it is.
I will have faith,
Through each wave.
I know that this,
Is now a part of me.
A part of me,
I will have to love and accept.
The intensity may fade,
As the larger waves roll in.
I carry this weight around with me.
I know that these waves will pass,
I know the tears won't stay.
I know the heaviness just means,
There was so much love in my heart.
So much love,
I was giving away.
This grief just means,
My heart is large.
My heart was full.

My heart is pure.
This grief just means,
I am capable of love.
This grief just means,
That my love has no place to go.
This grief.
This wave.
I will have to let it go.
It cannot stay,
It will need to flow.
The sensation is here,
And then it will leave.
How much longer?
When will it be over?
Have patience,
And listen.
Feel it,
And Surrender.
This wave won't stay.
The pain won't last.
Let your grief in,
Feel it pass.

Find The Love

Find the beauty.
Find the color.
Find the softness.
Find the clarity.
Find it all,
In the confusion.
Clarity and confusion,
It really is a thing.
Because it is in the confusion,
That clarity comes.
It is in the chaos,
That we find peace.
It is in the darkness,
That we find light.
It is in the wounds,
That we find healing.
It is in the numbness,
That we find emotions.
It is in the hardship,
That we find what comes easy.
It is in the fear,
That we find love.
We carry all of this along.
We learn to walk through the hard stuff.
We learn to carry,
All of these stones.
We learn to empty.
We learn to lighten.
We learn to make our load lighter.
Put the stones down.

Get rid oft the weight.
We make mistakes.
We find failure.
We fall down.
We can stay down,
And drown.
Get back up.
Always,
Get back up.
There is always light ahead,
No matter what.
It is in the failures,
That we find success.
It is in the drowning,
That we come back up for air.
That air is always refreshing,
And light.
That air that we breathe in,
Will fill us back up.
That air is love.
Find the love,
As you come back up.

The Bad Boy And The Good Girl

The bad boy meets the good girl.
He was the bad boy.
He seemed to get any girl he wanted.
They fell,
All over him.
She was the good girl,
Not knowing anything,
She was so naïve.
She had never seen the world.
This bad boy meets this good girl.
He thought he could play his game.
The same way,
He always did.
It was almost too easy,
The way he would work it.
Until he met her.
He played the game.
He was meticulous.
It was like he had a schedule.
He knew just what to do.
Until it didn't work.
It didn't work,
Not on her.
She would not be put off.
She would not be ignored.
She would be respected.
She would be treated well.
She would not be controlled.
She would not be used.
She would not be betrayed.

He only knew,
Just one way.
He only knew,
That one way that worked.
Until he met her,
She would call him out.
She would tell him how it was.
She would make him look at himself.
She would speak the truth,
And then live her life.
She didn't fall all over him,
Just like all the other girls did.
She was the one girl,
He couldn't have.
She was the good girl,
And he was the bad boy.
She wouldn't give her heart,
Because she knew his past.
She treaded lightly,
And would never trust him.
He walked away,
From every girl.
He never gave his heart,
And never let anyone in.
She was capable of giving her heart.
She had done it before,
She could do it again.
But won't go that route.
Not until,
He can prove himself.
Prove to her,
That he can hold her heart.

Treat her heart with care.
Let her be who she wants to be,
And say what she wants to say.
Prove to her,
That he can open up.
Prove that he can take a risk.
Put himself out there,
Without running his script.
Be real for once,
Open his heart.
Quit acting like a narcissist.
Vulnerability.
He wouldn't go there,
He wouldn't give her that.
He didn't make her feel safe.
He wouldn't open up,
Not about the deep stuff.
It was mostly all about him.
He didn't want to deal with love.
So, they kept playing this game.
Sometimes they were friends,
And sometimes, they were more.
They couldn't get along,
No matter how hard they tried.
It always ended,
In a fight.
They couldn't last,
More than just a couple days.
The truth would come out,
And he would yell,
Or he would run away.
She let him run.

She let him go.
She let him run,
All over town...
With any other girl.
She would never let him speak to her,
In a way that he always did before.
He had this temper.
He had this anger,
That he wouldn't face.
He'd put it on her,
And she would leave.
That is not okay,
She will not stay.
He would have to change his ways,
Become someone new.
But could he do this?
Could he figure this out?
He hated that he had,
This attraction.
To the one girl,
He just couldn't have.
And she hated,
That she cared.
About the one guy,
Who would never commit.
Her heart was closed,
And so was his...
And this was just,
What they did.
They had this flame,
That never burnt out.
This chemistry remained,

No matter what.
Why did she care?
When he wouldn't stay.
Why did she care?
When he wouldn't let her in.
What was this draw?
Why them?
He would leave,
But could never stay away.
They continued this process,
For many years.
They brought out the worst,
In each other.
Are they helping to heal,
The wounds that they both have?
Is this what their attraction,
Was all about?
Or, Was this a trauma bond?
They were very similar,
Yet so different.
He was the bad boy,
Who didn't care.
And she was the good girl,
Who cared too much.
They were both strong personalities,
And very independent.
Capable and strong.
Good at being on their own.
They were both good,
At running away.
He would leave,
And she would block.
They would play these,

Ridiculous games.
They were both rebels,
They both had that side.
He would test her,
And she would put him in his place.
She would test him,
And he would put her back in hers.
They were both doing the very same thing.
Running in circles,
Repeating this pattern.
They both wanted proof,
That this would be worth it.
They were both scared.
They had both been burned.
These games,
Were all because of their wounds.
This flame,
It was confusing.
It wasn't healthy.
It wasn't working.
They were both fine,
Living their lives.
So, what would it take?
For this to all change?
This is a question,
She just can't answer,
And neither can he.
This is a game,
She ended...
Once and for all.
Once she found,
Love for herself.

The Fixer

It is them.
It is them.
It is not me.
Everyone else has a problem,
That I need to fix.
I don't need to fix myself.
It is them.
Not me.
Blame everyone else.
Focus on everyone else,
Takes the focus away from me.
Fixing everyone else,
And being needed,
Makes me feel worthy.
Let me fix you.
Let me help you.
Let me be there for you,
And never for myself.
I don't know any other way.
I am the fixer.
I am the helper.
Let me go support you.
Let me jump when you need me.
If you need to be fixed,
I will be there.
If you need to be helped,
I will be there, as well.
I need to be needed,
That is my purpose.
This is because,

I have a void.
Inside of myself.
A void,
That I don't want to look at.
Let me distract myself.
Let me run away from it all.
Let me surround myself,
With people,
Who need me all the time.
This is how I found my worth,
For a very long time.
Focus on everyone else.
Focus on who needs me.
Where is there a project for me?
Who needs help,
I know how to fix you.
This is who I thought I was.
This is how I lived.
I didn't have real relationships.
Because this was the foundation.
Me, the fixer.
Me, the helper.
Me, the scapegoat.
Me, the people pleaser.
Me, with no voice.
Me, with no boundaries.
Me, with no worth.
Me, with a void.
But once I started,
To see myself.
I started to realize,
That this was not me.

This was who I was expected to be.
This was who I thought I was supposed to be.
This was a role.
That I was put in.
Without my permission,
Without my consent.
This was who I was told to be.
This was a role,
I fit into so well.
This was how I felt worthy.
This was when,
I put my worth,
In someone else's hands.
This was before.
All before,
I took my power back.
This was before,
I saw myself.
This was before,
I saw my soul.
This was before,
I heard my little girl,
Calling out.
She told me,
That was just a role.
It was all fake.
I can un-do all of this.
I can un-make myself.
I can change.
It is allowed.
And I am in control now.
So that is what I did.

I changed my role.
I changed how I felt worthy.
I had to look inside of myself,
To find all of this out.
I took control,
Of my worth.
I will decide who I am.
I will decide now.
It is me,
That decides,
I am worthy.
It is me,
That decides,
My role.
My new role,
Is simple.
It is me.

I Couldn't Save Him

I couldn't save him...
So maybe I can save you.
I couldn't save him...
So, I'm hoping I can save you.
I couldn't save him...
This broke my heart.
I carried this with me.
Around with me.
I just wanted to save him.
I learned this was not my job.
This was not my responsibility.
But it broke my heart.
I wanted him back.
Back the way he was.
So maybe I can save someone else,
If I couldn't save him.
I loved him so much.
I still do.
I want the best for him.
I always will.
I want him happy and healthy.
No matter where he is.
I sacrificed my whole being,
To try to save his.
I made myself sick,
To try to save him.
I honestly believed,
That I could do this for him.
If I could just figure everything out...
Everything out for him.

If I found him a therapist,
He would go and get better.
If I found a treatment center,
He could go and come back for us.
If I found a way to save him,
He would want to save himself.
I couldn't save him...
So maybe I can save you.
Until the day I realized,
This is not my job.
My job is not to save anyone.
I cannot do that work.
I cannot save anyone.
I can only save myself.
And now I know...
It is up to him to save himself.
I knew I was healed,
When I believed this wholeheartedly.
That job is for him...
For him to save himself.
This is his problem.
This problem is not mine to carry.
My job is me,
And he needs to save himself.
He did not worry about me,
While he was out caring about himself.
He did not think about how his behavior...
How his behavior was affecting me.
He did not think of me,
While I was feeling unsafe inside.
My whole world crumbled,
And he did not stay to help.

Help put it back together.
He did not stay to help fix it.
Help fix this crumbled world.
This crumbled mess around me.
Everything was a mess.
And he just left.
It was about him.
He couldn't see it.
He couldn't see this mess.
This mess that he made.
He just couldn't see it.
This is why it's a disease.
A disease that takes them away.
I couldn't save him.
Only he could do that.
Why was I the one sacrificing myself,
To help fix his world?
Why was I the one doing this work?
Because he could not see.
He just simply could not see.
It was not my job to get him to see.
The only job I have,
Is me.

It Is *How* People Love You

It is not what people do for you.
It is not what people say.
You can do and do and do for me.
You can say all the nice things that you want.
I have learned this lesson.
This lesson,
That came with a lot of reflection.
I have watched.
I have observed.
I have learned.
I have learned,
That it is *how* people treat you.
It is *how* people love you.
It is the checking in.
It is in the listening.
It is in the questions.
It is the support.
It is giving me the space,
That I ask for.
It is giving me the space,
If that's what I need.
It is in the small things.
The small things,
That make a difference.
Those small things,
They go so far.
It is how people love you,
Behind your back.
It is how people love you,
When you have been kicked down.

It is in those small,
Tedious actions,
That you see who people are.
It is what is behind those actions.
Are you genuine?
It is how a person responds,
To what you have to say.
It how a person responds,
When you are real with them.
It is how a person responds,
When they don't get something they want.
It is how a person responds,
When they don't get their way.
It is how a person responds,
When you tell them something they don't want to hear.
It is how a person responds,
When you call them out.
It is how a person responds,
When you hold them accountable.
Can you apologize?
Will your actions change?
It is in those actions,
That you start to see.
That is when you see your people.
The ones who are meant to be.
The ones who are meant to stay.
Those are the ones.
You can be so nice to me.
You can give me the world.
But if you don't allow me to be me,
Then what's that say about you?
I need to say what I need to say.

I need to be honest.
I need to be truthful.
I need to not walk on eggshells.
If I say something,
And you make it about you.
This tells me,
That you're not really listening.
Your focus is on you,
Not on me.
It is how you hold space for people in your life.
When I ask you to be accountable,
And you brush it aside.
That's okay,
But I can't have you in my life.
It is important to me,
To have the right people.
It is important to me,
To have accountability.
It is how people love you.
It is in that how.
That how,
Will take a while to see.
That how,
Is not immediate.
That how,
Takes time.
That how,
Won't show, right away.
Give it time.
Just wait.
Eventually,
You will see,

How people love you.
Let them show you.
Let them be.
Let everyone just be.
Let them be who they are.
Organic and natural.
We are all learning.
We are all just learning.
We can choose to have an open mind,
Or we can choose to close it.
It is those with that open mind,
That are open to learn.
We all make mistakes.
We are all human.
We all mess up,
From time to time.
We aren't going to act perfect.
No one is perfect.
It is in that open mind,
That we learn from our mistakes.
It is in that how.
How do we learn?
How do we learn from our mistakes?
How do we love our people?
What do our people need?
How can I love you?
How can I learn?
It is in that how.
It is how people love you.

This Comes With Love

My heart.
It is so sensitive.
It is open.
It loves.
Treat it gentle.
Treat it with care.
Treat it like it's yours.
Please don't break it.
My heart.
It's here.
It's beating.
It's breaking.
I've learned that our hearts,
Will break over and over.
It just means,
We love so much.
Our heart will break,
And then we repair it.
Our heart breaks,
Each time we grieve.
Each time we grieve,
Our heart is different.
Our heart will let go,
Over and over again.
Our hearts are made to love.
Our hearts are made to break.
Our hearts are made to grieve.
Our hearts are made to mend.
This is a process.
We will have to learn.

Learn our hearts.
Learn the care.
In order to love,
We will have to lose.
Lose and grieve.
This comes with love.
My heart.
It feels.
It feels it all.
I feel the love.
I feel the grief.
I feel the joy.
I feel the sadness.
I feel the light.
I feel the darkness.
My heart.
It loves.
It loves,
Fully.
It loves,
Completely.
It loves,
With everything.
It just loves.
My heart.
It loses.
It grieves.
It breaks.
It rips open.
This is what comes.
Comes with love.

This is what comes,
When you love,
Fully.

Spreading The Love

Turn the ugliness,
Into beauty.
Turn the darkness,
Into light.
Turn the grief,
Into love.
Pass it along.
Spread it out.
Turn the Voids,
Into a space.
Into a space,
For self-love.
Into a space,
For loved ones.
Loved ones who are here,
And loved ones who have left us.
Turn the pain,
Into forgiveness.
Turn your ego,
Into your soul.
Feel this sadness,
That is here.
Feel this pain,
I promise it won't stay.
Leave little trails of beauty.
Leave little pathways of light.
Open our hearts,
And follow the love.
Lean into the hardships.
Lean into the emotions.

Lean into the darkness.
Lean into the grieving.
Lean into letting go.
Lean into connecting.
Lean into vulnerability.
Lean into it all.
Spread the love.
Spread your heart.
Spread the support.
Spread your soul.
Give it to the world.
Just keep,
Spreading the love.

Feel These Waves

Feel this misery.
Feel this pain.
Feel this darkness.
Feel this wave.
Feel this wave of grief.
Feel it for however long you need.
Feel it because it's heavy.
Feel it because you loved.
Feel it because you loved so deeply.
This wave is here,
For you to feel.
This wave is here,
To be acknowledged.
This wave is here.
This wave of grief.
It's okay to feel this sadness.
It's okay to feel this loss.
It's okay to feel your heart hurt.
It's okay to feel this space.
This space is for grief.
This space is for the love that you had.
This space is for the heaviness.
This space is for the wreckage.
Be a mess.
Let it out.
Grief never looks a certain way.
Grief isn't here to have you look beautiful.
Grief isn't here to have you act nice.
Grief is messy.
Grief is heavy.

Grief is debilitating.
These waves are here.
Feel these waves.
Waves of anger.
Waves of denial.
Waves of bargaining.
Waves of depression.
Waves of sadness.
Waves of acceptance.
All of these waves.
Let them come.
If they come all at once,
Feel them.
If they come separate,
Feel them.
Please don't rush.
Please don't push them away.
Please don't bury them.
These waves,
Let them come.
Discomfort and agony.
Misery and suffering.
Grief is transformation.
Love that is transformed.
This love that you had.
This love that you felt.
This love that you gave.
This love that you held.
This love has transformed.
Transformed your soul.
Transformed who you are.
Transformed this love.

This grief that you feel,
It will not be pretty.
It might not be understood.
It might not be looked at,
The way it should.
You will want others to understand.
You will want to let others in.
You will want others to see your grief,
The same way you see it.
You will want it to be received.
You will want it to be heard.
You will want each wave,
Understood.
Seen.
Received.
Grief is so messy.
Grief is so dark.
Grief is a rollercoaster,
That many will never understand.
Many won't see you,
Through your grief.
Many want you,
The way you were before.
Before the chaos.
Before the waves.
Before the weight.
Before the darkness.
This grief will transform you.
These waves have affected your heart.
Feel these waves.

Deep Feeler

To be a deep feeler.
It means feeling it all.
Feeling into the depths,
As you fall.
Feeling the light,
As you rise above.
A deep feeler,
Will absorb it all.
Absorb what's around me.
Absorb what is in you.
I will meet you where you are.
I will never try to take away your pain.
I will listen and support you in your downfall.
I will hear your pain.
I will meet you there.
I have been there.
I have fallen,
Into those depths.
Depths of darkness.
Depths of pain.
To be a deep feeler,
It means we have experienced pain.
It means we have experienced waves.
Waves of grief.
Waves of light.
Waves of pain.
Waves of love.
Deep pain.
Deep sorrow.
Deep agony and sadness.

This deep, dark energy flows throughout me.
To experience the deep darkness,
Is to experience deep love.
I love so deeply.
Love so deeply.
To love is to rise.
To love, is also to fall.
Falling and rising.
This dance of balance.
I must go down,
To get back up.
The depths of darkness.
The depths of light.
This light is love.
This darkness is pain.
These wide ranges of emotions must be felt.
I must go into the darkness,
To experience this light.
I rise to fall.
I fall to rise.
The ups and downs.
It all must be felt.
To have my heart open,
Means to experience it all.
I will feel this love.
I will feel this pain.
I will honor my fall.
I will honor the rise.
I will honor whatever feelings surface.
My feelings surface,
So, they can be honored.
Honored and adored.

My feelings come up,
So, they can be seen.
They must be seen.
They must be heard.
My feelings are here,
Hold them all.
Hold them.
Love them.
Please don't dismiss them.
These feelings may bring discomfort in others.
This discomfort they feel,
Is not my concern.
Those that dismiss my feelings,
Are probably dismissing theirs as well.
To dismiss.
To ignore.
Ignore the darkness.
Ignoring the darkness,
Is to ignore the light.
Once you acknowledge and feel this pain.
This pain will transform,
Because it has been seen.
This agony.
This misery.
It will transform.
Transform into beauty.
Transform into light.
Nothing is permanent.
Feelings are temporary.
These deep dark feelings,
They will come...
And then they will leave.

These deep dark feelings,
Are my guidance to healing.
Pay attention.
Trust and surrender.
Make sure to feel.
Feel these emotions.
Grieving is real.
This grief,
I feel.
This is real.
I will fall into my emotions,
So that I can come back up.
I will let myself fall,
So that I can learn.
Learn to rise.
Rising from the depths of darkness.
Rising from experiencing loss.
Learning to ride these waves of grief.
These waves have a peak.
Rising at the peak,
And then falling on your way back down.
These waves,
Are needed.
Needed for my healing.
Me,
The deep feeler.
The riser.
The faller.
I have learned to ride these waves.
Coming up,
Falling down.
Rising above,

To fall once more.
Sometimes these waves,
Come crashing down.
Sometimes these waves,
Come with a violent sound.
Sometimes these waves,
Cause more conflict.
Conflict and resolution,
Through these waves.
These waves are crashing.
These waves are loud.
These are the waves.
The waves in me.
The waves,
Of a deep feeler.

My Father Wound

These selfish men.
They put themselves first.
They won't admit.
They won't take responsibility.
God forbid,
They take accountability.
They say they have integrity.
But where is it in their actions?
They use their words well.
They talk a good game.
Their words reeled me in.
They are filled with words.
But where is the action?
The only action I see,
Is lack of accountability.
The only action I see,
Is that they can't follow through.
The only action I see,
Is what is best for them.
The only action I see,
Is when they leave.
They are good at that.
They are good at leaving.
They leave when it gets hard.
They leave when they are called out.
They leave when they have shame.
They can't tell the truth.
They can't be a man.
They can't face their fears.
They can't face their wounds.

They run from themselves.
The only action I see,
Is what is good for them.
Whatever is good for them,
Is what they decide.
They can use their words,
To get what they want.
But they can't use their words,
To communicate their needs.
To communicate with me.
Communication is missing,
When it doesn't suit them.
But to get what they want,
They communicate all day.
These manipulative men.
They only use words.
They use their words,
For their own gain.
They use their words,
To play their game.
But when it comes time.
Time for serious.
Time for genuine.
Time for commitment.
They don't know what to do.
The ones who are filled with shame.
They hide.
The ones who don't have worth.
They leave.
I've put myself aside,
For men like this.
I've put myself aside,

To please these kinds of men.
These are the men that I was drawn to.
Drawn to them.
Because of my dad.
Because of this wound that I have.
Because of this father wound.
This wound that I am aware of now.
This wound that I will close.
This wound that I will heal.
I will take care of myself.
I will take care of this wound.
I will take care of my pain,
Within this wound.
I will honor myself.
I will honor this wound.
I will honor my self-worth,
By putting myself first.
Never sacrificing myself,
Not ever again.

Pretty Words

Tell me,
Everything I want to hear.
Tell me,
How wonderful I am.
Pretend to be,
Someone you are not.
These pretty words,
Are here again.
Predict the future.
Lure me in.
Make me feel safe,
In the moment.
Tell me,
Everything I want to hear.
Tell me,
How you feel.
Love bomb me.
Made up feelings,
You are telling me.
Because you don't know yourself,
Or how you are feeling.
You are disconnected,
From yourself.
So, you come up...
With pretty words.
You speak from your ego.
These pretty words make you look good.
These pretty words make you feel good.
These pretty words make you a "man".
This is what you think being a man really is.

A man of his word.
A man of integrity.
This is what you say that you are.
These are all just pretty words.
Because you can't back them with action.
You can't follow through,
No matter how hard you try.
Because you avoid yourself and your inner work.
You push your feelings,
Right away.
And then they come out,
Bleeding onto everyone else.
Bleeding onto me,
Who has accepted your words.
Your pretty words excuse your actions.
This was me,
Over and over.
This was me.
Excuse your behavior.
Excuse it every time.
Because you promised this,
And you promised that.
Please.
Please.
Please.
Mean it this time.
Please just mean what you say.
Please?
For me?
All I ever wanted.
All I wanted was to believe one word.
I wanted you to mean,

One word you said.
I wanted to believe.
Believe in at least one man.
But once again,
All it is.
Is a pretty word.
You cover your actions with pretty words.
Your pretty words are all that you are.
A man of action,
Is not in the cards.
A man of his word,
But only pretty words.
Fake words.
Good words.
Only good.
False promises.
Apologies that mean nothing.
It's all about you.
Genuine and honest,
Are not in your vocabulary.
It is always me,
Processing your actions.
Trying to figure out what you really mean.
Trying to make sense.
Make sense of it all.
Trying to make sense of why I have you in my life.
All I ever wanted.
Was a man.
A man to believe in.
A man to keep me safe.
A man to protect me.
A man of action and integrity.

A man with self-worth.
A man who actually means what he says.
A man of consistency.
A man of self-love.
A man who stands up.
Stands up for himself.
Stands up for his values.
Stands up for his beliefs.
Stands by his pretty words,
And what he says to me.
A man who doesn't walk away,
After feeding me pretty words.
My little girl.
She has this wound.
This wound, that was made using pretty words.
Pretty words from men,
Who have let her down.
These pretty words.
She has learned.
Learned to be manipulation.
This wound of manipulation.
This wound of pretty words.
This wound will be healed,
With genuine action.
This wound will be healed,
With honesty and truth.
This wound will be healed,
With consistency.
This wound will be healed,
Using truthful words.
Pretty words won't be used,
To heal this wound.

These pretty words.
They made this wound.
This wound in her,
That has affected her trust.
This wound will close.
This wound will heal.
This wound remains open with pretty words.
She no longer accepts pretty words.
She no longer hears them.
She no longer entertains them.
She has walked away from any pretty word.
Any pretty word that is said to her.
She no longer accepts this,
In her life.

Narcissist

Gaslighting.
Dismissal.
Words that put me down.
Make fun of me please.
Shut me down.
Project all of your shit.
All of your problems,
Put them on me.
Please, go on this power trip.
Your reality is the only right reality.
My feelings don't matter,
Only yours do.
You are always right.
Your way is the only way.
Manipulate and string along.
To meet all of your needs.
You have your little crew.
Your little crew that defends you.
Your little crew that doesn't see you,
For who you really are.
They have been manipulated.
They have been fooled.
Fooled by the master.
This master is you.
You hold all of the power.
You are in control.
You triangulate and victimize.
The victim is always you.
You are the martyr.
You are never at fault.

You will turn it around.
You will always find blame.
Blame it on someone else.
Blame it on me.
It is always my fault.
Shut down my reality.
My opinion doesn't matter.
You are not open to hear,
What I have to say.
You don't care.
You never will.
The only person who matters,
Is yourself.
You are not open to change.
You are not open to hear.
You are not open to learn.
You are not open to share.
Share your vulnerabilities.
Because you are so perfect.
You look for gossip,
All over town.
You want the juicy news.
You love when others are down.
You thrive when I have a problem.
You thrive when I am kicked down.
And when I pick myself back up,
You are always there to kick me back down.
I can rely on you for this.
I can rely on you to knock me back down.
I rely on myself,
To get back up.
I finally get myself back up,

And here you are again.
You arrive just in time.
You arrive to make me feel good.
Feel good, just for a second.
This actually has more to do with you.
Making me feel good,
Strokes your own ego.
Making me feel good,
Has nothing to do with me.
That would involve you having empathy.
Love bomb and idealize.
Then come the put downs.
Devalue me please.
This is what you do.
Then discard me.
Throw me away and drop me.
Like I never mattered in the first place.
Then, this pattern begins again.
This is the pattern that becomes my life.
My life of narcissistic abuse.
My life that you are in control of.
You are in control.
You hold the power.
I let you have ownership and possessiveness of me.
I am an object.
An object to use.
Use for your own personal satisfaction.
An object to make you look good.
Make you look good on the outside.
It is always how it looks.
How it looks to everyone else.
But on the inside.

The inside of my life.
It is hell and control.
Put downs and neglect.
Emptiness and loneliness.
Abandonment and confusion.
Loss of myself,
Each and every time.
Every time I let you back in.
Every time I have you close.
Anytime I depend on you.
I will satisfy your every need.
I don't know who I am.
I don't have my own identity.
I don't have a purpose.
A purpose without you.
Without your control.
This is the way you want it.
I am an extension of you.
You have conditioned my worth,
To depend on you.
You have conditioned me,
To meet your needs.
This is my job.
This is what I do.
This is my role.
My role for you.
My role is not to please myself.
My role is not to become who I am.
My role is to serve you,
And that is it.
It is time.
Time to see.

Time to see you,
For who you really are.
It is time to walk away.
Walk away from you.
Walk away from this game.
Walk away from this abuse.
This no longer works.
Works for me.
I have finally found my worth.
My worth that you have kept me from.
Kept me from seeing.
I have found my worth.
I no longer need you,
To bring me down.
I no longer need you,
To kick me back down.
I no longer need you,
To control me.
I no longer need you,
To manipulate and blame me.
I no longer need any of this.
I am walking away.
"No, thank you."
"Goodbye."
I am walking away.
This time for good.
I finally know my meaning and purpose.
I finally understand where I belong.
I finally understand what my future holds.
And none of that includes,
You.

Hopefully

He swept her off her feet.
He took her in his arms.
He told her all good things.
He put on the show.
This show was for her.
This show was to get her.
He waited for her to bring down her walls.
He waited for her to say it all.
Spill her heart.
Tell him her flaws.
He waited for her to open her heart.
He waited for her to give him her all.
He waited for her to build him up.
She built him up,
So that he felt good.
And once he got,
All that he wanted.
Once he was built up and felt good.
He looked at himself,
And knew it was her.
It was only because of her,
That he felt like this.
He knew deep down.
He was no good.
He knew deep down.
He couldn't keep up.
Keep up with her.
So, what does he do?
Self-sabotage this.
He stands up.

And then.
Just like that.
He said,
"No. I'm good. I'm all set."
He looked down at her.
Her, so vulnerable.
Her, with no power.
Her, with her open heart.
He turned around.
And just like that.
He dropped her.
He left.
And stomped all over her heart.
He would soon blame her.
Put the blame on her.
"You must not act that way."
He said.
Whatever he needs,
To make himself feel better.
Whatever he needs to do,
To cover up his shame.
She knows this.
He showed her.
He showed her,
Who he really is.
So, in the end.
It is her.
That says,
"I'm actually all set."
In the end,
It was her that walked away.
His loss.

His mistake.
To treat a girl this way,
Is just not okay.
Hopefully he learns.
Learns his lesson.
She hopes he never does this again.
Does this to another girl.
Girls deserve respect,
And hopefully he learns.
He learns to respect the female body.
He learns to respect a girl in his presence.
Hopefully he grows into a man.
Hopefully he can learn accountability.
Hopefully he finds his integrity.
Hopefully he learns what respect looks like.
Hopefully he learns,
It is not all about him.
Girls have feelings too.
They have needs too.
Hopefully he learns,
To listen and make space.
Hopefully he learns to become her safe place.
Hopefully he learns,
To treat her emotions with care.
Hopefully he learns,
It is not all about him.
Hopefully,
He learns.
Hopefully.

Let Me

Let me get this.
Let me get that.
Let me make you think,
I am so into you.
Let me make you think,
You are the only girl.
Let me make you think,
I am the guy for you.
Let me treat you good.
Let me text you all day.
Let me call you every morning.
Let me call you every night.
Let me buy you flowers.
Let me be there when you need me.
Let me lure you in.
Meanwhile,
I am doing this.
With 6 other girls.
Maybe more.
Maybe 2 more.
All while I am doing this,
I am feeding my own ego.
My ego is so large.
I am in a good place.
I am so great.
(So, I think.)
Until it all falls apart.
Until you figure me out.
Along with the other 5.
I am down to only 2.

Thank God, I still have my ego.
Let me go find 4 more.
So that I can still play my game.
Let me do this,
For my whole life.
Until it all falls apart.
And I am left with nothing.
I really can't apologize.
I really can't mean it.
I really can't make up for my poor behavior.
I won't be given another chance.
Another chance by the one who stood by me.
The one who actually cared.
The one who actually was there to help me.
Help me,
When everyone else left.
Help me,
When I was in a bad place.
I will have to sit in this.
I will have to actually realize this.
I will actually have to look at myself.
Look at all the harm that I have caused.
I made a mess.
I can't clean it up.
I deserve where I am.
I know she is right.
They are all actually right.
I just don't want to admit.
I really don't want to look at any of this.
I just want to move on with my life.
Shrug it off.
Shove it under the rug.

Let me keep going.
So that this will spill onto more girls.
All because,
I don't want to feel.
All because,
I don't want to see.
I don't want to admit any of this.
I don't want to realize this mess is mine.
I don't feel like cleaning it up,
Or making amends.
I really don't want to clean up this mess.
I will just run away.
Run away from it all.
How do I get out of this?
Out of this mess?
How do I reach myself again?
How do I leave my ego behind?
How do I fix this mess I made?
...Let me get back to you on this.

Let Me Fix You

Let me fix you.
Let me fix you.
Oh, and you too!
I will help fix you!
Oh, you need help.
You need me.
You need to be changed.
You are damaged,
Come to me.
You have problems,
I am here to solve them.
I am here,
To always listen.
I am here,
To fix your psyche.
Let me teach you how to be.
Let me teach you new ways.
Let me buy books,
For you to read.
So that you can fix yourself.
And I can help.
All of my dates,
Are interviews.
Interviews,
So that I know how to help you.
All of my dates,
You all tell me.
All of your problems,
I am here.
Date number one,

Tell me your past.
Date number two,
Dissect your wounds.
Date number three,
Figure out what you need.
Date number four,
I start to fix you.
By the end of a few more dates,
We are through.
All of our childhood trauma,
Has come up.
Go fix yours.
I will go fix mine.
Leave it to me,
To find anyone to fix.
Leave it to me,
To find someone with problems.
I am a safe space for your trauma.
Let me date you.
And you.
And you.
I see all of your problems.
By the way,
We all have problems.
This was part of my problem.
It is not up to me,
To fix any of you.
It is not up to me,
To take on your problems.
Problem solved,
On my end.
I am not here to fix you.

I am here to fix me.
And,
I am here to just be me.
I can understand your problems.
I can help empathize with you.
I can listen and understand.
Give you a safe space.
But other than that,
I am not here to fix.
I am not here to help.
Nothing to fix,
Just to be.

Please, Not Dinner.

Take me to dinner.
Take me out.
Let me get dressed up.
Let me do my hair.
I will even wear heels.
I will wear my dress.
I will go to dinner.
Dinner with you.
You will pay.
I will say thank you.
Wait.
Why am I doing this?
This is not what I need.
I don't need to be taken to dinner.
I don't need you to pay for my food.
This is not my idea of a date.
Why am I even going to dinner?
I can take myself to dinner.
I enjoy my own company.
I can buy my own food.
I don't even want to do my hair.
I really don't want to wear heels.
I'm certainly not wearing makeup.
I'm not going to a bar or getting a drink.
I don't even drink.
I don't drink alcohol,
I drink water.
Water and coffee.
Sometimes tea.
So, if you want to take me for a drink,

I will decline.
It's just not my thing.
I just want to be cozy and comfy.
I just want to sit on a blanket and eat.
I want to relax.
Be in the grass.
I want to be free.
Connect with the earth.
I would rather be on a picnic.
Sitting on a blanket.
Get takeout to go,
And sit on this blanket.
Good conversation.
We are connecting.
Enjoy this picnic.
Be outside.
Breathe in this fresh air.
Let my hair be free.
No makeup.
No heels.
Honestly,
No shoes.
I love my bare feet.
My bare feet on the grass.
My toes to be free.
I honestly hate shoes!
I want the lake or the water by my side.
Beautiful scenery is my idea of a date.
Sunny days.
Sunflowers.
Fresh air.
Feel the breeze.

Be out in nature,
That's my idea of a date.
Feel the warmth of the sun.
The warmth of the sun,
On my skin.
Take me on a boat.
Take me on a hike.
Or let's just sit,
And meditate.
Meditate outside.
Outside in nature,
Of course.
Or maybe let's go on a road trip.
I guess, if we have to be inside.
Let's go to a show.
Not a movie,
But a Broadway show.
Something musical.
Something theatrical.
Something artistic.
Just please,
Not dinner.
Let's go pick lavender.
Or go see the sunflowers.
Let's go see a psychic,
Or something spiritual.
Let's go to the beach,
Be down by the water.
Let's go make a candle,
Or can I watch you make music?
Get a massage.
Full body or a foot massage.

Let's do some self-care.
Let's go for acupuncture.
Let's be active.
Go for a bike ride.
Let's do yoga.
Let's go kayaking,
Get out on the water.
We can go see the animals.
Go to the zoo,
Or even better...
What dogs are at the rescue?
A pet store would be better than going to dinner.
Let's go for a walk.
Can I play with your dog?
Let's watch the sunset.
Or even the sunrise.
Do you want to wake up early?
We could do the sunrise and church.
Breakfast is better than going to dinner.
Breakfast means no makeup,
And my hair is not done.
Let's go for coffee,
Let's just relax.
Coffee shops are my favorite.
I also love to dance.
I am a free spirit.
I am different.
I like different.
I am not your average girl.
I love to be free.
Create our own dates.
The date for our mood.

Lost Herself

Spontaneous and being in the moment,
Over having a plan.
The sun.
Nature.
The beach and water.
Flowers and the earth.
I love to be active.
I love to just be.
I am not really needy.
It is just your quality time.
We can just sit,
And have conversation.
Connect with me,
That is all I need.
It is your time.
Your time that you give.
That is all I need, really.
Your time is our date.
(But can we please be outside?!)

More Than My Looks

I am more than my looks.
I have a heart.
I have a brain.
I have insides.
I am more than my looks,
Please see past all of that.
I am sick of being seen for my looks.
Looking at my body,
Can you go beyond that?
Appreciate me for who I am.
See me,
For who I am.
I am so sick of being looked at,
For my looks.
Can't you see that I am more than that?
I'd like to be respected.
Respected as a whole.
A whole person is who I am.
Ask me questions.
Find out about me.
Find out who I am,
I am more than what I look like.
The world can be shallow.
To me,
Looks are shallow.
The outside is nice,
But what is inside is nicer.
My insides are deep,
And if you can't keep up...
Please step aside,

I hate small talk.
A conversation tells me your intentions.
I can feel your intentions from the very first word.
I am extremely intuitive and can pick it up.
My emotions get in the way sometimes,
Of this gift.
Please look past what is on the outside,
I am so much more than what you see.
I am extremely deep.
And if you don't like it,
That's okay.
I can't live on the surface.
I love deep conversations,
And quality time.
I am an old soul,
And I live deep.
Deep in myself,
Is where I live.
So please see that,
Get past my looks.

Let's Be Open

Let's get deep.
I hate small talk.
Let's talk dreams.
Let's talk goals.
Let's talk real.
Let's get deep.
Deep in yourself.
I want to know.
I will tell you.
I will share.
Let's be vulnerable.
Let's be open.
Just share it all.
Why hide?
What's the point?
Just be yourself.
Don't hold back.
Just be you.
I am me.
I have good and bad qualities.
I will share them with you.
You share yours.
Let's just be real,
And honest, of course.
Deep conversations,
They are my favorite.
I love to talk deep.
I love to talk about feelings.
I love to be open.
Conversate with me,

I am here to listen.
I love to learn new things,
And hear your point of view.
How can I be better?
What do you have to add?
I want you to share your opinion,
But I don't really have to agree.
I just want you to feel safe with me.
I love new perspectives.
I love to hear how you've grown.
Who were you years ago,
And who are you now?
This is how I used to be,
And this is who I am now.
I love growth,
I love leaving what I knew,
To go where I've never been.
Oh,
This is hard.
This is OH SO HARD.
I am willing to go there though,
To be who I am supposed to be.
I will feel all the things.
I will let my old self go.
I will learn new patterns and new ways.
I will learn new beliefs.
I will share with you,
All of these.
So, tell me how you have grown.
My growth will help you.
And your growth will help me.
We have stopped to conversate,

And meet each other,
Along the way.
Along this path of life.
This path of life.
You have helped to mold who I am,
And I have helped you too.
I send love to all of you,
Who I have met on my path of life.
Even if our story didn't end well,
I still have love.
Love for you,
In my heart.

It Was Fine

He dated her.
For a little while.
He dated her,
And it was fine.
Nothing over the top,
It was pretty normal.
He was a pretty good boyfriend.
He would check on her.
He would call her and was consistent.
He treated her well.
He checked all of the boxes.
He had a good job.
He had a few houses.
He made good money.
He had an amazing family.
He had beautiful friends.
He made a life for himself.
He brought her,
Into his life.
He showed her his life.
He showed her his family.
He showed her what he would give her.
He even accepted her dog.
He was a planner,
And she wasn't.
His planning drove her nuts,
Because she wanted to just be free.
He was looking for someone else.
Someone she would never be.
She could feel this.

She observed this.
She just wasn't going to be,
Who he was looking for.
She would drive him crazy,
Because she would disappear.
She would go on road trips.
She just wanted to be free.
She didn't want a plan.
She didn't want to be locked down.
She wanted to run away,
And leave town.
She wanted her music up,
The sunroof down.
Her dogs face out the window,
Breathing in the fresh air.
Driving to God knows where.
She didn't have a destination.
She had no idea where she would end up.
He would call her,
And say, "Where are you?"
And she would say,
"I Don't know."
This was not the girl for him.
This was not the guy for her.
He liked everything just so.
His papers, perfect and all in order.
And when she would walk through the room,
All of his papers would fly up, everywhere.
Everything in disorder,
When she was near.
She would put the milk,
In a random place.

He was constantly moving it back.
Because,
"The milk goes here."
She never had a rhyme or reason,
For anything that she did.
He was so Type A,
Organized to the T.
Everything was so orderly.
She brought disorder,
To his life.
She brought some mix up,
To his perfection.
He even let her,
Put mismatched knobs,
In his kitchen.
Mismatched was not really his thing,
But he let her do it,
Anyways.
Him and her dog,
Didn't really get along.
They would argue sometimes,
Him and her dog.
He would get mad.
And so would her dog.
This was a stressor,
That was building among them.
This bothered her,
And bothered her dog.
This was a thing,
That was going on.
He was a good guy.
She knew he would make a good husband.

To a girl,
That just wasn't her.
She wasn't going to be,
What he was looking for.
She just needed freedom.
She wanted to be free.
He was looking to build a family.
She had to end it.
She had to tell him.
They said goodbye.
They parted ways.
This was a decision,
That benefited them both.
He was ready for his life to start.
And she still needed to go,
And figure herself out.

On Time

Oh, you're late?
You're late again?
Hasn't anyone told you,
To not keep a girl waiting?
Please don't be late.
Late for me.
I need you to be on time.
On time for me.
If you can't show up on time,
For just one date.
What will it look like for future dates?
The second date.
Late again.
Some excuse,
You apologize.
You take accountability,
Which I like.
Finally,
A guy who takes accountability.
Okay,
It's fine.
I let it go.
Please don't be late.
Late again.
Can you be timely?
Can you be on time?
Time is important.
Important to me.
It shows me,
How you show up.

It also lets me know,
If I am a priority.
If you can't show up on time,
And you are always late.
I am the one who is waiting.
My life is messed up,
Over here.
While I wait for you,
To finally show up on time.
How many times will we do this?
How many times will I accept this?
I really don't like late.
I am bothered by it.
Just say a different time.
A later time.
It also shows me,
That you are not a man of your word.
You say you will be ready at 7.
I trust in those words.
If you can't show up at 7,
The words you said are not true.
This affects my trust in you.
Especially when it is more than once.
Late more than once,
I just can't do.
I am annoyed now.
I don't want to go now.
I was ready 10 minutes before.
I have been ready,
Waiting for you.
Why am I the one waiting for you?
Waiting past the time you said.

I am still waiting,
As you text.
Your texts are this:
"I'm coming.
Hold on.
15 more minutes.
I'm still on a call."
I am annoyed by these texts.
I am annoyed before I even see you.
I am just annoyed,
That you are not on time.
On time for me.
On time for yourself.
You are the one who asked me to go.
Go with you tonight.
This was your idea.
You asked me.
And you can't show up?
Show up for me?
No, thank you.
I need you to be on time.
It's just how it is.
It's just how I am.
Please, please.
Be on time.

Ghosted.

We hang out.
We have a few dates.
We have great conversation.
We enjoy the time.
Good talks.
We kiss goodnight.
We talk every day.
You plan a date night,
And ask me if it's alright.
Once a week dinner.
We text every day.
I like what you talk about.
I like how you text.
You are really smart.
You are a great writer.
I love how you write.
You could write a book.
I tell you this.
There were a few problems,
We talked about this.
We had a conversation,
On the phone.
You basically told me,
What I wanted to hear.
You asked what a good day would be,
For me to see you.
You asked when I was free.
I told you these days.
You told me you would text me with plans.
Plans that were never made,

Because you ghosted me.
You didn't text me with plans,
There was no explanation.
I didn't hear from you again,
You just disappeared.
That is fine.
You do you.
If you don't want to talk to me anymore,
You were welcome to say it.
Communicate to me,
I feel like I deserve it.
Deserve a little something.
A little explanation.
Something.
It didn't even have to be a phone call.
But a text?
Say something,
Explain.
I am not sure what happened.
I was not given an explanation.
This was the time,
I was ghosted.

Time To Go

He opened the door for me.
He walked me in,
I sat down.
The next 2 hours,
He talked about himself.
He barely stopped,
To get a breath in.
He talked about himself.
He complained the whole time.
He complained the whole time,
About his ex-wife.
His ex-wife,
Who got sick.
With a fatal illness.
He complained about her.
He complained about this.
I sat there in disbelief.
That he couldn't see himself.
Does he hear himself?
Does he realize what he's saying?
Does he hear his words?
"In Sickness and in health."
Those were marriage vows,
I'm assuming he took.
She was really sick now,
This was a good time for him to leave.
He really said this.
Said this to me.
She was sick.
She couldn't help it.

She couldn't give him kids,
So, he must go.
He left her.
And now he is single.
Single,
Going on dates.
With still,
No kids.
No girlfriend.
No wife.
While your ex-wife is home.
Home, taking care of herself.
Home alone.
Home alone,
While she is deathly sick.
Home.
By herself.
Without you there.
And now you are sitting with me,
Telling me this whole story.
Don't you feel guilty?
Just a little bit?
You think I am going to want to see you again?
You think I am going to pick a man,
Who leaves his sick wife?
You think I am going to pick a man,
Who knows she is sick?
Taking care of herself.
While you sit with me,
Complaining about this?
How dare you.
How don't you see?

How don't you realize,
That this is repulsive?
Your behavior,
As a husband.
I really don't love.
I really don't know how you leave her,
To deal with this.
All on her own.
But that is not my problem.
My problem is,
Why am I sitting here listening to this?
I must get up.
I must go.
Get up to leave.
Get up and go.
It's time to go.

One Date

Do you want to go on a date?
Just one date.
Go to dinner.
Conversate.
Connect.
Just one time.
I'll never see you again,
After this.
After tonight.
Just this one date.
We'll see if we have a connection.
We will have a conversation.
A conversation,
I won't remember.
I will barely remember it,
When I think of it.
What did we talk about?
Where did we go?
What did we eat?
I don't remember,
Really.
I don't remember.
I do remember,
That you were late.
You shrugged it off,
Like it was nothing.
You took my picture.
Me with my food.
Why did you do this?
I barely know you.

I met you,
Only one time.
And now you have my picture.
Isn't this weird?
I smiled,
But when will this be over?
Why am I doing this?
Am I posing?!
Our conversation,
I am still trying to remember.
I really don't recall,
What we talked about.
I remember thinking,
What time is it?
When will this be over?
Is it time to go?
How do I get out of this?
I go to the bathroom.
I look at the time.
I decide.
It really is time to go.
The time is late.
Not really.
But it is time.
Time for this date to end.
I couldn't wait.
I couldn't wait for it to end.
I couldn't wait to get back to the table,
And tell him.
"It's late." I said.
"Time to go."
"It's only 8." He said.

"Right! 8 is late and I have to go!"
I really don't remember,
But I think I ran to the door.
I rushed to my car.
Hurry, get in!
I drive home.
Thank God.
Why did I go?
Thank God I am home,
In my own bed!
I go to sleep.
I slept really well.
The next morning, I tell him.
"There was no connection for me."
He calls me.
He sends me many texts.
More and more texts are coming in.
He calls me again.
He leaves a voicemail this time.
"I don't understand. Please pick me.
Give me another chance.
I felt a connection.
I want to create something healthy with you."
Oh no.
Please stop.
I hang up the phone.
Please don't say these words,
After just one date.
I block.
You are blocked.
I am freaked out.
It was one date.

Just one date.
And you called,
Begging me.
It was one date.
I can't.
I don't understand.
It was only one date,
And you are begging me?
It was one date.
That is all.
That was our one connection.
Please don't call.
You are now blocked.
And that is final.

Wrong Men

She went to the wrong men,
Because she just wanted to be loved.
She put up with so much,
Because she thought that's what love was.
She didn't trust herself,
So how could she trust them?
She lost trust in her gut.
She became enmeshed,
In trauma bonds.
Similar traumas is what they shared.
Similar roles.
Similar childhood experiences.
Similar,
In all the wrong places.
Their traumas were connected...
Forming an attachment.
This is not what love was.
She will keep going until she finds it.
More work on herself,
Needs to be done.
She was giving her love away,
And leaving none left for her.
She wasn't listening to herself,
Because she fell into her role.
Put their needs first,
What do they need?
That role is not her.
She needed to make peace,
With her inner demons.
She was drawn to the wrong men,

Because of what was inside of her.
She needed to go within,
And figure herself out.
She would learn the lesson.
This lesson from each one,
And keep moving forward.
Forward she would go.
She would start believing in herself.
She would listen to her gut.
She would check in with herself,
Instead of listening to everyone else.
They all have an opinion.
Their opinions fill her mind.
Their words get in the way,
Of hearing her heart.
Connect with her body.
The answers are found there.
Her body will tell her everything she needs to know.
Just have trust.
Heal her wounds.
Let go of everything,
Become her true self.
See these men clearly,
Without the illusion.
Change herself.
Change her beliefs.
Change her role…
Put her needs first.
She will stop trying to fix them.
That is not her job.
Accept them for who they are,
And that they are not for her.

These are the wrong men.
The wrong men for her.
Let it go...
Keep moving forward.
She needed to make peace with her past...
Connect with her true self.
Connect with her creativity.
Figure out what she wants.
She will become what she wants,
And attract that man.

These Walls

These walls I battle.
These walls are there.
These walls will come down.
I won't have them stay.
These walls I built,
Because I didn't feel safe.
These walls I built,
They are not needed anymore.
I have made my life safe.
I have made a safe space for me.
I have found safety,
For myself.
For my heart.
These walls,
I don't need.
I don't need them anymore.
Please let them down.
I feel like I am in a cage.
This cage kept me safe.
This cage was my place,
To come to feel safe.
This cage.
These walls.
They are not needed anymore.
Look at this life,
That I have built.
I have done this.
All by myself.
I left my old world.
My old world was,

Where I needed these walls.
These walls of protection.
This cage to feel safe in.
This cage is not for me,
Not anymore.
I need to be free.
Free from this cage.
Let these walls come down.
These walls are protection,
That I no longer need.
These walls are protection,
That are not helpful anymore.
These walls will cause damage,
In this new world.
Please bring down these walls.
I will do it for me.
Each time a wall comes down,
I must feel the pain.
Feel the pain,
That I couldn't feel before.
I couldn't feel,
Because I didn't feel safe.
The pain I was in,
When I built this wall.
These walls were built,
Out of pain.
These walls were built,
To protect me from this.
I must bring these down.
It's okay to feel.
It's okay to feel this now.
You are safe.

"I am so sorry,
That you experienced this."
"I am just so sorry."
I will tell myself this.
I am safe now,
To remove these walls.

I Will Cry My Eyes Shut

Tonight.
I will cry my eyes shut.
Crying so hard that I can't even think.
Crying so hard that I can't even feel.
My heart just hurts.
My heart is broken.
This radiating pain.
I am in agony.
Tonight.
I will cry my eyes shut.
My heart is crying.
Crying without you.
Without you by my side.
How could you hurt me like this?
How could you leave me like this?
How could my heart ever feel like this?
Tonight.
I will cry.
Cry all night.
Cry my eyes shut.
So many tears.
Tears in my eyes.
I have never cried.
Cried like this.
How could you hurt me like this?
I just don't understand.
Where did you even go?
My heart knows that you left.
My heart knows the love that I had.
The love that I had for you.

My heart knows.
My heart is broken.
These tears are for you.
This pain is for you.
My heart.
My eyes.
My tears.
Tonight.
These tears.
I will cry my eyes shut.

Fear

This fear.
I feel it in my stomach.
I feel it in my chest.
I feel it in my throat.
It's burning.
It's intense.
It's all over.
It wakes me up.
It weighs me down.
It's haunting.
It comes with negative thoughts.
Get out of my mind.
I need to shut off my mind.
Breathe.
I am back in my body.
I feel this sensation now.
What is worse?
The sensations?
Or the thoughts?
It'll pass.
The fear won't stay.
Feel the fear,
And move along anyways.
Breathe in.
Breathe out.
Stay here.
Stay in it.
This is completely valid.
This fear.
It'll pass soon.

This fear makes me want to stay.
Stay where I've always been.
Not go, where I want to go.
Leave that comfort zone.
Bring the fear.
The fear will come.
All alone.
Me with this fear.
On our way.
Moving forward.
This fear will bring bravery.
That'll be my reward.
That'll be the end zone.
The fear won't stay.
It's just here.
Now.
It's not permanent.
Stay present.
Trust and surrender.
This fear will take me over,
If I don't just let it flow.
Okay.
Flow through me.
I'm okay with it now.
I know what it is.
And I know it won't stay.
Just a wave.
To come over me.
Just a wave.
A wave of fear.

The Men In Her Life

How could you?
Why did you?
Did you know what you were doing?
I am finally sad.
Sad for myself.
I am sad for her.
I am sad that the men that she had in her life.
I am sad that they betrayed her.
I am sad that they were cowards.
I am sad that they affected her trust.
I am sad that they didn't keep her safe.
They didn't protect her.
They protected themselves.
These men,
They showed her.
Showed her their true colors.
They couldn't be a man.
They didn't have worth.
They didn't believe in themselves enough,
To be able to stand in their masculine traits.
They didn't protect her,
When she needed it the most.
They took her safety completely away.
The men in her life.
They did this to her.
The men in her life,
Have proven to her.
They have proven that they can't protect her,
Or have her back.
The men in her life,

Have treated her like shit.
The men in her life,
Have proven they don't stay.
They have proven,
That they can't care for their emotions.
They have proven,
That they will leave.
They will leave when things get hard.
They will leave,
When she voices her needs.
They will leave,
When she stands up to them.
They will leave,
When she feels an emotion.
They are not comfortable with her emotional capacity.
They are not comfortable with her emotional sensitivity.
These men in her life,
They have proven to be weak.
They have proven,
That they don't want her to speak.
They don't want to hear her words.
They don't want to hear what she says.
They don't want her to speak the truth.
They don't want to be held responsible.
They won't take accountability.
They won't apologize.
They won't change their actions.
They won't change their behavior.
They are filled with shame,
And so they leave.
They leave because they are weak,
And can't be a man.

Lost Herself

These are the men,
That she is drawn to.
These are the men,
That have been around her.
These are the men that she is used to.
These are the men that she knows.
This is what is familiar.
Familiar to her,
Because of what she looked up to.
She looked up to men like this.
These were the men,
Who were her role models.
These were the men,
That were supposed to take care of her.
These were the men,
That were her caregivers.
These were the men,
That hurt her.
These were the men,
That were cowards.
These men were easily controlled.
Either controlled,
Or controlling.
Easily influenced.
Easily manipulated.
Or they were the ones,
Who would manipulate others.
These men chose themselves,
Over her.
These men chose to live in their trauma responses.
These men can't deal with their own emotions.
These men put their anger on her.

These men use her for their needs.
These men have proven.
Proven to her,
That she doesn't even know what a real man is.
She doesn't know,
Because she has yet to see it.
She has yet to learn,
What a real man is.
What are the qualities?
What does it feel like?
What is it like to be heard?
What is it like to have a man care?
What is it like to have a man come through?
What is it like to have a man who doesn't come first?
She doesn't know.
She has yet to see.
She has yet to see a man,
Come through for her.
She has yet to believe,
In a man again.
She used to believe.
She used to have faith.
She used to love,
With her whole heart.
She gave these men her love.
She gave them her word.
She was there,
To help them.
She was there,
To appreciate them.
She was there,
To support them.

She was there,
To lift them up.
She was there,
To give them faith.
She had faith in them.
She believed in them.
They took it all.
They took it with them when they left.
They used her,
To fulfil a need.
A need in them.
All of these men,
This is what they did.
They did to her,
Without a second guess.
They took and took and took from her.
They only gave,
For their own gain.
They used their charm.
They used their money.
They used their words.
They put on a show.
The next thing she knows,
She is betrayed.
She is abandoned.
She is left.
She is beaten down.
She is destroyed.
These men,
They have affected her.
These men,
Have helped her see.

Helped her see,
What she will not accept.
She will no longer accept,
A man acting like a coward.
She will no longer accept,
A man who acts like a child.
She will no longer accept,
Emotional unavailability.
She will no longer accept,
A man calling himself a man.
She will need him to show her.
Show her,
With his actions.
When a man can come through.
When a man can match his words with his actions.
When a man can protect her.
When a man can give,
Just to give.
When a man provides,
Without having expectations.
When a man can give her a safe space,
For her emotions.
When a man can feel.
Feel his emotions.
Feel them in a healthy way,
And has his own outlets.
When a man can regulate himself.
When a man can believe in himself.
When a man has self-worth.
When a man has self-love.
When a man has it handled.
When a man can stand in his divine masculinity.

When a man can be a man.
This is when,
She will let him in.
Until then,
She will work on herself.
She will work on her own masculine.
She will thrive in her feminine.
She will be emotionally open.
She will work through her own emotions.
She will work through her own trauma.
She will work through her wounds.
She will find her worth.
She will see why she has attracted these men.
And when she is ready,
She will be emotionally available.
Emotionally available for a man in her life.

She Wasn't Ready

He texted her.
He called her.
He was direct.
He acted like a gentleman.
He opened her door.
The car door every time.
He treated her well.
He asked her questions.
He was a good guy.
He wasn't a creep.
He was a family man.
He had a good job.
He knew exactly what he wanted.
He had himself together.
And she wasn't ready.
Ready for him.
She wasn't ready for the good guy yet.
She wanted to have fun.
She wanted to go on dates.
She came across like the wild one.
She was so free.
Wild and free.
She came across like she didn't care.
But this was how she kept herself safe.
She wanted to do,
Whatever she wants.
Whenever she wants.
She was pretty flaky.
She didn't want to commit.
She didn't want plans.

She didn't want closeness.
She didn't want him.
She wasn't ready for the good guy.
She was annoyed,
When he cared for her.
She wasn't ready for him to respect her.
She didn't allow him to get too close.
And if he did,
She would run.
She wasn't ready.
Ready for this guy.
The guy who put her first.
The guy who treated her well.
She wasn't ready,
To fall in love.
She wasn't ready,
To bring anyone close.
She had her walls,
To keep him out.
She just needed herself.
She needed to learn to love herself.
She needed to learn to put herself first.
She needed to learn to trust herself.
She had been beaten down.
Down to the ground.
She needed to come back up,
By herself.
She just wasn't ready.
Ready for the guy.
The guy who would allow her to fall,
Safely in his arms.
Because when she falls,

She falls hard.
When she falls,
She falls deep.
She wasn't ready for this guy.
She wasn't ready for him to make her his all.
She wasn't ready for a commitment.
She wasn't even ready for a companion.
She just needed space.
Space to be.
Space to be her.
Space to be free.

Emotional Shutdown

Emotionally shut off.
She was shut off from her emotions.
She was shut off from herself.
She shoved it all down,
To not feel her stuff.
She was shut off from the world.
She shut herself down.
She shut off her emotional side.
She became emotionally withdrawn.
She suppressed it all.
She suppressed her pain.
She suppressed her tears.
She suppressed it all,
To move on with her life.
Her emotions were never accepted.
Her emotions were never treated with care.
Her emotional side,
Was always dismissed.
Her emotional side,
Was never heard.
Her emotional side,
Became a burden.
A burden to everyone around her,
That couldn't hold her emotions.
Became a burden even to herself.
She didn't even know how to hold her own emotions.
Everyone around her,
Couldn't get in.
She felt like she was a burden.
She needed to build walls.

Walls to feel safe in.
This became her way.
Her way of coping.
Her way of dealing.
She needed to shut herself down.
Shutdown because she didn't feel safe.
She will build these emotional walls.
Walls to protect her.
Walls to keep her safe.
She will build these emotional walls.
They will keep everything out,
And away from her.
She will never allow anyone to hurt her,
Like she was in the past.
Hurt before.
Hurt in her past.
Her past was hurtful.
Her past was painful.
Eventually,
She would have to face it.
Face her emotions.
Face her pain.
Face what happened.
What happened to her.
This is what she knows,
To build these walls.
This is what she knows,
Is to keep everyone out.
She will become her own safe space.
She will learn to hold her emotions.
She will let herself feel,
As soon as she feels safe again.

She will move away,
From those who don't make her feel safe.
She will move away,
From others with emotional walls.
These walls,
She can feel.
These walls,
Are familiar.
She knows these walls.
She understands.
She understands why they must have these walls.
The others who have walls,
They are not good for her.
She needs to be around,
Those who are emotionally open.
Emotionally open,
Is good for her.
This is what she needs now.
This is where she feels safe.
She feels safe with emotions.
She feels safe when others are open.
She can't relate anymore to walls.
She can no longer be emotionally shut down.
She can no longer be emotionally shut off.
She can no longer be emotionally withdrawn.
This won't work for her.
Not anymore.
She wants to be open.
She wants to be free.
Free from the walls.
Free from the pain.
She wants to be emotionally open.

She loves her emotions.
She loves her sensitivity.
She loves this side.
She now knows how to thrive,
In her feminine side.
She has embraced her feminine.
She has repaired her masculine.
She is now officially,
Emotionally open.

Let Yourself Be

Let yourself be sad.
It's okay.
Let yourself feel.
Let yourself be.
Let yourself see.
Let yourself love.
Let yourself be whatever you need to be.
I am just sad.
Sad today.
I am so sad.
I am in grief.
I have let go.
Let go of so much.
I have known so much loss.
So much loss,
To me.
It didn't make sense.
Make sense at all.
Why am I here?
Why do I have to feel this?
I remind myself,
This is part of my journey.
I am here.
Here to feel.
Here to heal.
Here to move on.
Move forward.
Keep going.
Keep moving ahead.
It's okay to be sad.

Be sad today.
It's okay to be sad.
It's okay to grieve.
It's okay to feel this.
I am sick of this.
I am sick of this feeling.
I am sick of this grief.
I am sick of this healing.
This is how I feel.
How I feel today.
This is just today.
This is just right now.
Every moment is different.
Take it one step at a time.
Take it one second at a time.
Take it one minute at a time.
Take it one day at a time.
Pick one of these.
For your quote of the day.
Whatever you need,
To get you through.
Whatever you need.
Let yourself be.
Let yourself be whatever you need to be.
Just be here.
Just be here now.
Right now,
You are sad.
This is okay.
It's okay to be sad.
It's okay to cry.
Just be here.

Just be here now.
Just feel.
Feel.
Feel.
Feel.
Feel this grief.

This Wonderful Day

This wonderful day.
I imagine this day.
I feel so much love.
Love that is around.
Around me.
This wonderful day.
I imagine this day.
This day needs to come.
Please come,
Soon.
This wonderful day.
I pray for it.
Happiness.
Joy.
Bliss.
And warmth.
This day.
I imagine.
This day after healing.
This day after this journey.
This journey of darkness.
This wonderful day.
Smiles and laughter.
No more worries.
No more pain.
No more loss.
Enjoy this day.
This wonderful day.
I imagine this day.
This day will come.

I will keep this vision.
In my mind.
I will hope for this.
In my heart.
I will pray for this day.
This wonderful day.
This day is waiting.
Waiting for me.

Numbing

This numbing.
Oh.
This numbing.
I don't want to feel this.
This pain I am in.
Oh.
This hurts.
This really hurts.
This agony I am in.
I just want to numb.
I would rather numb.
Numb this pain.
I would rather numb this pain,
Than to feel it.
I am letting myself feel.
Feel this loneliness.
I feel all alone.
This pain.
This misery.
This is so hard.
Hard for me to feel.
Hard to sit in.
This reality is here.
Staying in the moment,
Right now is hard.
I am here in this moment.
And this moment is hard.
This moment hurts.
This moment really hurts.
This loneliness I feel.

It's okay.
I am in it.
This moment, that is here.
I hear you.
I see you.
This feeling, I acknowledge.
Please move through me.
Move through my body.
Move through me now.
Please leave.
Thank you for telling me.
Telling me that you are here.
This feeling... it hurts.
I hear all of my limiting beliefs.
This voice I hear,
It is not mine.
This voice is the one,
Telling me to numb.
This is not what I need.
What I need is to feel.
I hear you.
I see you.
This feeling, I know.
I know you are here.
Right now, you are here.
I am ready to feel.

Dear Wounded Masculine & Feminine

Dear,
Wounded Masculine.
Dear,
Wounded Feminine.
I am trying to balance.
Balance both of you.
I am trying to find balance,
Between the both of you.
I would like to heal you.
Both of you.
I would like you to be in your divine.
I would like you to be balanced.
I would like you to be healthy.
I would like to heal your wounds.
Your wounds in both of you.
Dear Wounded Masculine.
Dear Wounded Feminine.
I now understand how this happened.
I now understand where the root is.
I now understand how you have been bruised.
I now understand how you have been wounded.
I understand now.
I have taken the time.
I have taken the time to sit with you.
I have taken the time to hear you.
I have taken the time to see you.
I want to understand you.
I have taken this time.
I have gotten to know,
Both of your sides.

I have seen in action,
These wounded sides.
I have been living,
Through these wounded parts.
They have been showing up.
Showing up in my relationships.
I see you.
I hear you.
I understand.
I am listening now.
I am paying attention.
I understand that they have been destructive.
I understand now,
Where this has come from.
I understand now,
How you became damaged.
I am here to heal and repair.
And give you love.
Dear wounded masculine.
You don't have to be all in your mind.
I will heal my feminine side.
This way you feel grounded.
Please don't become cold and distant.
I want you to feel present and of service.
Please don't become selfish.
I want you to feel giving and providing.
Please don't become controlling.
I want you to feel supportive.
Please don't become critical.
I want you to feel non-judgmental.
Please don't become fearful.
Fearful of failure.

I want you to feel confident and accountable.
Dear wounded feminine.
You can end your people pleasing ways.
I want you to inspire others.
Inspire others to shine.
You no longer have to tolerate toxic people.
You can now set loving boundaries,
And speak your truth.
Your low self-worth is now replaced.
Now replaced with knowing your worth.
You are worthy, and you know it.
You no longer accept external validation.
Your validation now,
Comes from within.
This voice within you,
Is soft and loving.
She is understanding and compassionate.
She is no longer aggressive.
Your negative self-talk is now replaced.
Replaced with speaking gently to yourself.
You are kind to yourself.
You are compassionate now.
You now allow and let things be.
No more forcing.
No more pressure.
You have learned surrender.
You are creative.
You are intuitive.
You are nurturing and loving.
You can embrace your darkness,
Without becoming the victim.
You no longer suppress any of your emotions.

You commit to feeling and being emotional.
You no longer sacrifice yourself for others.
Your needs come first.
You love being assertive.
You enjoy your confidence.
You embrace vulnerability and express your emotions.
You have become authentic.
You have stopped being passive.
You have stopped being needy.
You have found trust in yourself.
You have found your open heart.
You are reflective.
You are empowered.
This letter to you both,
I hope finds balance.
I need you both to balance each other.
Being balanced,
You will feel a sense of harmony and fulfillment.
I need your wounds to heal.
I would love to stand in my divine.
My complete divine masculinity
Alongside
My complete divine femininity.
I would love for you to both be balanced.
I would love for you to both be healed.
This letter to you both,
Thank you for listening.
Thank you for healing.
It is now time to leave your wounds behind.

I Have Learned To Stay

I didn't allow myself to get sad.
I didn't allow myself to cry.
I wouldn't allow myself to feel this pain.
This pain inside.
This agony.
This huge void,
Deep within me.
Letting go of our love.
Letting go of your love.
Letting go of our hearts.
Our hearts that were connected.
Our hearts.
Our love.
How could you leave?
How could this have happened to me?
This disbelief.
This hollowness.
This space.
This void.
This deep dark hole.
I filled it up,
With everything.
Everything other than my own love.
I ran away.
Ran away from it all.
I have been running,
All this time.
Find an escape.
An escape for me.
All I ever wanted,

Was to be happy.
Find happiness for myself,
And live my life.
Find my purpose.
Find my meaning.
I couldn't find any of that,
While I was running.
Running from myself.
Running away from this pain.
Running away and escaped.
Escaped myself.
Escaped my pain.
I ran away from this void.
I ran away from the truth.
My protection was an illusion.
This illusion was not true.
This was my protection.
This kept me safe.
I couldn't see reality.
All I knew was to run.
Keep running,
From myself.
My heart is large.
And when I love,
I love deep.
My heart,
It broke.
And I had no idea,
What I would need.
I didn't know.
I had no idea.
All I knew,

Was to run.
Run away.
It's what I do best.
Run away from pain.
Run away from love.
Run away from my heart.
Run away from my soul.
I am coming back.
I turned around.
And learned to stay.
Learning myself.
Learning my pain.
Learning my heart.
It's time to heal.
It's okay that I ran.
It is all that I knew.
I am here now.
I am here with myself.
No more running,
I have learned to stay.

I Read The Room

Always reading the room.
My nervous system ramped up.
On high alert.
What is your motive?
What do you want?
Hypervigilance is my gift.
I read the room,
On high alert.
I don't trust you.
Not yet.
I need to feel you out,
Show me your flaws.
Once you show me who you are,
I will decide if you are safe.
Safe for me.
To have in my life.
I will read the room.
How do you deal with conflict?
Do you have a temper?
Are you here to manipulate me?
Are you here with strings attached?
Are you using me,
For your own gain?
Why are you here?
Are you here for me?
Or are you here for you?
Is this about me?
Or is this about you?
Relationships are a two-way street.
You do you.

I do me.
We get to know each other slowly.
It is not a race.
A race to the end.
A race to a specific outcome.
Life is not a race.
Life is a journey.
A journey of different speeds.
Getting to know someone is sometimes giving space.
Honoring boundaries and your needs.
Honoring my boundaries and my needs.
Do you listen when I speak?
How do you cope?
Do you live in survival mode?
Hypervigilance is my gift.
I will pick it up,
If you are not being genuine.
I will pick it up,
If something is off.
Authenticity is my life now.
Show me your true genuine self.
We all make mistakes.
We are not perfect.
Admit our flaws and our weaknesses.
Closed minds are out,
Growth mindsets are in.
Being fake is in your past.
Speaking your truth is now.
Hiding who you are is no longer your life.
Leaving behind old ways.
Leaving behind what doesn't work.
And, I will continue to read the room.

Silence

Silence and solitude.
Peace and serenity.
Quiet the noise of the world.
It is in silence,
That I found myself.
It is in the solitude,
That I could finally breathe.
It is in the quiet,
That everything came.
Everything I shoved away,
For so many years.
I could finally hear.
Hear my own voice.
I could finally connect.
Connect to my soul.
It is in the peace,
That I could sort through the chaos.
It is in the in between,
Where I could think.
It is in the stillness,
That my body found safety.
Safety to feel.
My mind/body connection came to me.
Came to me when I was calm.
I found myself in complete stillness.
I listened to myself when it was quiet.
No more distractions.
No more noise.
No more plans.
No more influence,

From other people.
Just hearing my own voice.
Discovering meditation.
Connecting to my soul.
Feeling my feelings.
Releasing and letting go.
Letting go,
Of all that I know.
It is in stillness,
That I found clarity.
It is in my solitude,
I could see so clear.
Clarity and answers.
Answers to my questions.
Questions that went unanswered for so many years.
I found resolution to so much conflict.
Conflict with myself.
Conflict with others.
I found forgiveness.
I found acceptance.
I found compassion.
Compassion for others,
But mostly for myself.
It is when it became quiet,
That I nurtured myself.
It is in the silence,
That I heard my needs.
I heard my feelings.
I heard my voice.
I had to remove all of the noise.
The noise was keeping me from myself.
The noise was becoming such a distraction.

Lost Herself

A distraction from myself.
A distraction from my soul.
Avoiding my pain.
No more noise.
Only stillness.
Quiet and peace.
Serenity and bliss.

Betrayal

Betrayal.
Let me tell you what betrayal feels like.
It is like your heart is ripped right out of your chest.
It is like something rocked my whole world.
It is like my whole world is gone.
My whole world.
Ripped away from me.
My love for you.
Ripped right out of me.
My whole world,
Doesn't have meaning.
Everywhere I look,
Nothing has meaning.
How could my love for you,
Be so suddenly ripped away?
How could I be disappointed,
Yet again?
One day you are here.
The next day you are gone.
One day you love me.
The next day you leave.
My heart.
Is broke.
My heart.
Destroyed.
This pain.
This grief.
I can't describe.
Betrayal.

Betrayed.
A pain in me.
I just cannot even begin to explain.

She Had This Anger

She had this anger.
This anger in her.
She didn't know how to express it.
She didn't know how to get it out.
She had never yelled,
Or come undone.
She felt like she would appear unleashed.
Would she be called the crazy one?
"You must not feel."
"You must not be angry."
"Keep it all together,
You must do everything with a smile."
She kept it all in,
And no one even knew.
No one knew,
This anger in her.
This rage.
This anger.
It was starting to leak out.
YELL.
SCREAM.
GET FUCKING MAD.
She still didn't know how.
How to get mad.
She didn't know where to begin or where to start.
"I don't know how to even get mad," she said.
She said this with tears streaming down her face.
This is when I stepped to her and said,
"Please get mad. Whatever you need."
No one ever showed her,

Where to start with her anger.
No one ever told her,
It was okay to be angry.
She was taught to always be perfect,
And quiet.
Never make a peep.
Never start problems,
Keep it all in.
Be responsible for everyone else,
While they put their anger on her.
They would yell at her,
And she would never yell back.
Until the one day,
She did.
Until the one day,
She put them in their place.
She argued back,
She spoke the truth.
She raised her voice as she stood up.
She put her hands over her head,
While she yelled.
Yelled at them.
She was MAD.
She was angry.
And you know what they did?
They put her down and scolded her,
And told her to sit down.
They told her to get out,
"GO TO YOUR ROOM."
Ever since that day,
She kept her anger in.
She went to her room,

And didn't come out.
She didn't come out,
For a very long time.
She kept shoving her anger down.
Shoving her rage so deep down.
She walked around with a smile.
She appeared totally fine.
Until the day,
She stopped.
Until the day,
She accepted her anger.
She let it come out.
She will finally learn to be angry.
She will finally learn to yell.
She will learn that anger is okay.
She will learn that anger needs to be expressed,
And never kept in.
She will learn that she can come undone,
Because anger is healthy.
She will learn that anger is part of who she is.
She will learn to love her anger.
This anger in her,
Will finally come out.

Detach

Detach from this.
Detach from that.
Detach from it all,
Even an outcome.
Nothing has to happen at the end.
Everything will happen, just because.
Just enjoy the journey of it all.
The road less taken.
My path.
My journey.
Walk each step.
Complete each step.
Breathe in.
Breathe out.
Keep calm.
Detaching is exhausting.
Time to rest.
Nurture your body.
There is no end.
You know what you want.
And you will get there.
But right now,
Live for this moment.
Live for now.
Detaching from an outcome.
Detaching from a plan.
Detaching from, "you must do this."
"You must do that."
"Have it figured out."
"You must have a plan."

Detaching from pressure.
Detaching from being harsh.
Harsh on yourself.
Be kind to yourself.
You are on a path.
Step by step.
There is no rush.
There is no finish line.
There is no outcome.
There is just right now.
Once you detach from it all,
All you will feel is this path that you are on.
Evolution.
The rise.
The fall.
Money.
Fame.
Success.
Detach from it all.
Follow your heart.
And grieve the old.
Grieve what you had.
Grieve who you were.
Let go of a plan.
Let go of the outcome.
How it's supposed to happen,
Is in surrender.
Trust and detach.

Lost Herself

You Are Not My Friend

Oh, you think you know me?
You think you know me enough,
To talk about me?
Talk about facts that aren't even true?
You want to talk about me,
And my life?
When you have no idea who I even am?
Do you have any idea of what I was going through?
You are not my friend.
A friend does not do that.
I was a friend to you.
I picked you up when you were down.
I defended you when you weren't around.
"Those facts," you told.
Those were not facts.
"Those facts," were not true.
"Those facts," were a lie.
You call yourself my friend.
You play nice to my face,
All while you are ruining my name.
I have heard this smear campaign,
And supposedly it came from you.
You say you are my friend.
You are not my friend.
Please don't talk about me behind my back.
Please don't talk about my life,
Like you know.
Like you know me.
You don't even know me.
You don't know the real me.

You never will,
Because I did not let you see.
Let you see the real me.
So please take my name right out of your mouth.
And please next time,
Before you state facts.
Run them by me,
First.
Otherwise, it's gossip,
I don't approve.
Approve of gossip.
Words that are not true.
This is genuine gossip.
These words you spoke about me,
These words were not true.
I don't appreciate being talked about.
Especially by someone,
Who doesn't even know me.
You are not my friend.

Condescending

Oh, are you talking down to me?
Oh, you think you're better than me?
You think you know more.
You think what you have to say,
Is most important.
You interrupt me when I am talking.
You give me degrading nicknames.
Giving unsolicited advice,
As you assume you know it all.
The queen of backhanded compliments,
As you talk down to me.
The way you treat me,
Like you are on top.
Like you are better than me.
Thinking you are better than me.
Treating me,
Like the ground you stand on.
Treating me,
Like the ground to walk on.
This condescending behavior,
Is here.
I just want to let you know,
I see this behavior.
I am not tolerating it anymore.
This condescending behavior,
Has nothing to do with me.
This is you,
Covering up all of your insecurities.
Instead of being honest.
Instead of being authentic.

Instead of coming out,
To be completely open.
This is how you are covering it all up.
Argumentative,
You always have to be right.
Shooting down my feelings,
As you belittle me.
Constant interruptions,
In the middle of what I am saying.
You don't care what I have to say,
Because all that matters is what you say.
"Oh, it was just a joke?"
"Oh, you want me to take it easy?"
Yeah,
No thanks.
I am done being treated this way.

Autopilot

Cruising around on autopilot.
That is the way.
Hurry.
Hurry.
Hurry.
Just go.
Go.
Go.
Unaware,
Checking off all the boxes.
Get everything done.
Cruising around life in autopilot.
Not looking around,
At anything else.
Just focused on the task.
Go.
Go.
Go.
Get it all done.
Not enjoying the journey.
Just another box to check off.
Not in your body.
It is just,
Go.
Go.
Go.
Unaware of others.
Unaware of you.
Unaware of your actions.
It comes across as self-centered,

Because everything is so fast.
Going full blast,
Getting everything done.
Not getting a breath in.
Not sitting down,
Just for a minute.
Not enjoying the skyline.
Not noticing the sunrise.
Not taking the time,
To take in the beauty.
The beauty around you.
The sky is so pretty.
Cruising around life in autopilot.
Not feeling your feelings,
Unaware of your body.
Not taking rest...
It is time to rest.
Your body will speak.
Your body will talk.
If you don't listen,
Your body will yell.
Getting out of auto pilot,
Means connecting with your heart.
Connecting with your body,
That is where you can start.
What is your body saying?
Listen closely and get yourself out.
Out of autopilot.

She Left The Noise

She will speak her story.
She will speak her mind.
She has released her fear.
Her fear,
She's had.
She finally knows.
Knows the truth.
She finally understands.
Understands the truth.
She will no longer be manipulated.
She will no longer be led on.
She will no longer be buttered up,
To meet their needs.
She will no longer take on.
Take on the burdens.
The burdens of others,
Everyone else around her.
These burdens are theirs.
Theirs to carry.
Theirs to work through.
Theirs to hold.
She is not the one.
Not anymore.
She can't carry their burden.
This burden is theirs.
She will no longer carry.
Carry a weight.
This weight has been in her,
For so many years.
Guilt trips and punishments.

Projections that are not hers.
Projecting onto her,
is no longer okay.
She will move away.
Move away from this.
Projections and feelings.
Feelings that aren't dealt with.
She will no longer be a distraction to their problems.
She is not a distraction.
Please deal with your shit.
She no longer can be around any of it.
She will start to live her life.
Her life for her.
Her life she has not lived.
Because she lived for everyone else.
She will now hear herself.
She will listen closely.
She will listen to her inner voice.
She finally hears it.
She couldn't hear it,
Because of all the noise.
All the noise,
That was going on around her.
For so many years.
This noise prevented her,
From hearing herself.
Hearing what her needs are,
Hearing where she wants to go.
This noise.
Distractions.
Distractions filled her life.
Distractions became the noise,

That kept her from herself.
She shoved herself down.
She chose the noise.
She chose the distractions,
Which became her world.
Her world of distractions.
Her world of noise.
This noise.
This chaos,
Kept her away.
Kept her away for far too long.
She needed quiet.
She needed solitude.
She needed to hear herself.
Hear herself,
Finally.
This is where she needs to be.
This is where she belongs.
She gave this to herself,
As she left all the noise.

This Transitional State

Walking around.
Around this new world.
Walking around,
As this new girl.
This new girl.
My new self.
No one knows me,
Not anymore.
I have been in this cocoon.
This cocoon for myself.
This cocoon.
This chrysalis.
This transitional state.
I have removed,
Any attachment.
Any attachment,
That I have ever had.
Detach from it all.
Disconnect from everything.
This leaves,
Only myself.
This transitional state.
This state that I am in.
Detox it all.
Detox my body.
Detox anything old.
Detox the past.
Detox the pain.
Detox the weight.
Become fulfilled.

Fulfilled with love.
Fulfilled with joy.
Fulfilled with myself.
This transitional state.
This state that I am in.
I am still becoming,
As I let everything go.
Let everything go.
In this cocoon.
Silence and solitude.
Quiet and peace.
Calm and serenity.
This beauty inside of,
This transitional state.

Control

I have given up control.
I have given up my plan.
I will surrender to it all,
And accept what will come.
I am not in control,
Not anymore.
I used to think I had control.
Control of it all.
Control of myself,
Is pretty much it.
Anything else,
I have no control.
Just let everything be.
Let everything go.
I know what I want.
I know what I need.
The plan I have,
May not be what is.
There is a plan,
That is not mine.
I am not in control.
Control of the plan.
There is a God,
Who knows the plan.
I have surrendered to that.
What is meant for me,
Will be.
What is meant to happen,
It will happen.
What is going to be,

Will just be.
Everything will end up,
Just as it's supposed to.
I can't control what is meant to be.
I can only control me.
I am learning this.
It feels so free,
To give up control.
It feels so light,
To trust in a plan.
A plan that is not mine.
A plan that can't be controlled.
I am free.
Free from control.
Oh,
How I love this.
I am so free.
I am out of this cage,
I was in for so long.
No more control.
I am done with that.
I trust in the plan,
That is meant for me.
I will not force.
I will not control.
I will just be.
Be here now.
I am here.
I am free.
I get to be me.

Follow Your Heart

Take a risk.
Follow your heart.
Listen to your gut.
Your gut is right.
That gut.
That feeling,
It doesn't lie.
It will bring you to your life.
The life you were meant to live.
Listen to your gut.
You will know when it comes.
It comes to lead you.
It comes to guide you.
It is here to tell you.
Tell you when you are going down the wrong path.
Listen for the signals.
This feeling comes to put you in the right direction.
Listen closely.
Your gut is correct.
Follow this feeling.
Follow your heart.

I Became Wise Because I Fell

I am wise because I fell.
I fell to the ground.
I fell off the cliff.
I fell.
I kept falling.
I almost drowned.
I fell to the lowest,
That I have ever felt.
I fell to fall,
To rise again.
I stopped breathing for a while.
I kept on falling.
Falling to get back up.
Get back up again.
I fell to find,
Wisdom there.
I found wisdom at my lowest.
I found wisdom when I lost it all.
I found wisdom when I couldn't see.
I could not see,
Anything.
I could not see,
Anything ahead of me.
I could not see,
The good in this.
The good in this fall.
The fall,
I fell.
I found wisdom,
When I fell.

I found wisdom,
When I had nothing at all.
I found wisdom,
When I was not treated right.
I was not treated the way I should have been.
Wisdom was waiting for me at the end.
After I saw.
After I learned.
I picked up wisdom,
As my reward.
I found wisdom,
After each risk.
Risking my all,
As I fall.
I fell to the ground.
I fell to my knees.
I became wise,
In my demise.

My Heart Is Heavy

My heart is heavy.
Heavy today,
Heavy right now.
My heart feels grief.
Letting go.
Letting go of so much.
Parts of me,
My whole world.
This grief is real,
This wave is here.
This wave.
This grief.
This grief,
Today.
Parts of me,
I will let go.
I can't hold on,
Not anymore.
Keep moving,
Through this pain.
Through this heaviness.
This is grief.
Grieving my life.
Grieving the old.
Getting to know,
Unconditional love.
Carry this grief.
This grief with me.
I will carry it,
Everyday.

Learning to walk with this grief.
I carry this with me.
I honor this.
I honor this grief in my heavy heart.

I Feel You Still

I feel your spirit.
I feel you near.
I feel your eyes.
I feel your presence.
I feel you still,
By my side.
I feel your love,
In the air.
I feel you close.
I feel your distance.
I feel your energy.
But you are so far.
Far away.
Away from me.
This doesn't make any sense.
You are here.
But you are not here.
I see you.
But I can't see you.
You have transformed into my heart.
Your presence is with me.
I hold you close.
I imagine you.
Like you are here.
Here with me.
You are here with me.
Your soul,
I feel.
We are connected.
Our spirits.

Our love.
Our soul connection.
The love I had for you.
Has transformed.
It has transformed into grief.
I will feel this grief.
Each wave is here.
Each wave I feel.
This grief I feel.
This grief is love.
It is love,
I had for you.
I feel you still.
I feel your love.
I feel your heart.
I reach for you.
I am reaching for you.
But I just can't reach.
This distance I feel.
This is my grief.
I feel you still.
I always will.
I won't say goodbye.
I reach for your spirit.
I hold it close.
I pull it back,
Into my heart.
That is where you will be.
That is where you will stay.
You are here,
Inside of my heart.
You have transformed.

Transformed for me.
This is what I need.
I need from you.
I need you here.
I need you still.
I need to remember.
I will never forget.
I hold you here,
Your soul is close.
Your soul lives on,
Inside of me.
I feel you still.
I won't let go.
Your presence lives on,
Inside of me.
Your place is here.
Here with me.
Here in my heart.
I feel you still.
I hold you here.
Here with me.
You are here with me.
Always.
I feel you still,
By my side.

A Reminder Of You

Anywhere I look.
It is a reminder.
A reminder of you.
A reminder of our love.
Anywhere I go.
It is a reminder.
A reminder of you.
A reminder of our love.
Anything I do.
It is a reminder.
When I wake up.
It is a reminder.
When I go to bed.
It is a reminder.
As I go through life.
It is a reminder.
Life feels so empty.
Empty without you.
I feel this void.
This void in my heart.
Life is so quiet.
Quiet without your noise.
Quiet without your breath.
Quiet without your presence.
Life feels like it doesn't have meaning.
Meaning without you.
Meaning without you by my side.
By my side,
Is where you belong.
Right here with me,

In my life.
In my life.
In our life.
Our life that we had.
Our life that we lived.
Life as I knew it,
With you by my side.
By my side,
Is what I knew.
I have to let go.
Let go again.
Let go once again.
This is what I do.
Love to let go.
Let go of you.
Let go of this life,
That I knew with you.
Let go of the noise,
That I knew with you.
Let go of our routine.
Our routine,
We knew.
Let go of any reminder of you.
This doesn't mean I will forget.
This doesn't mean you are not in my memory.
This doesn't mean you lose your place,
In my heart.
This place is yours.
All yours.
Forever.
This doesn't mean I will forget.
All it means,
Is I will accept.

I will accept,
That you are not here.
I will accept,
This emptiness.
I will accept,
Your presence has transformed.
I know that you,
Want me happy.
I know that you,
Watch over me.
I know that you,
Are not truly gone.
I know that your spirit,
Lives within me.
I know that you would want me,
To let go of these reminders.
To let go of these reminders,
Is to be at peace.
Be at peace with this.
Be at peace with you.
Be at peace that you are resting.
Resting, at last.
I want you at peace.
I want you resting.
I want you happy.
This will be my new reminder.
This reminder.
That you are at peace.
You are resting,
In your happy place.
I will create a new reminder.
A reminder of you.

Courage

Embracing who we were always meant to be,
Is something that all of us can find.
We are all on this path,
to discover our true selves.
It is having the courage to go inside.
Inside, within.
Inside of ourselves.
It is there,
That we have everything we need.
It is there,
That we find courage and strength.
It is there,
That so many won't go.
Because it is there,
That we have to learn to flow.
Flow through the good,
and the really, really bad.
Connect to our body.
Commit to feel.
Commitment to feeling.
Feeling our emotions.
It is inside of ourselves,
That is the only way to grow.
We cannot be the same as we always were.
It is part of life,
That we change and move on.
We must find the courage,
To keep going.
Keep moving forward.
Keep going and going.

The past will try to pull us back,
Into whom we once were.
Courage to move on,
Is leaving what we know.
Sometimes it is,
Disappointing and leaving who we love.
It is a choice,
Not all of us make.
But the ones who do,
Commit to themselves.
The old way was to people please.
The old way was to always appease.
The old way was to sacrifice.
The old way was never using our voice.
We must find a new way,
As we move on.
Our new way can be,
Anything.
Anything we want.
Anything we choose.
It is up to us,
To decide.
It is finding our own voice,
That some may find hard to hear.
Our truth that is told...
Not everyone will agree.
But it is in our truth,
That we become FREE.
Free of who we thought we were.
Free of everything we thought we should be.
Free of anything holding us back.
Keep moving forward,

It will all shed away.
Our truth that is told,
Starts a whole new identity.
This is when we find ourselves.
Finding courage,
Doesn't mean that we don't feel fear.
It just means that we can feel the fear,
And we move forward anyways.
Feeling fear...
It is not bad.
Sometimes it means,
We're on the right track.
We can learn to walk,
Side by side,
With this fear.
Take this fear,
Take it along.
It is on that walk,
That will be up and down.
It is on that walk,
That we find the unknown.
And it is in that unknown,
That we find growth.
It is in that growth,
That we find the strength.
It is in that strength,
That we let ourselves be seen.
It is when we are seen,
That we can be loved.
It is when we are loved...
That we find meaning and purpose,
For this life that we live.

We must be real.
We must be seen.
We must be heard.
Once we find ourselves,
Everything will fall into place.
Like the law of attraction,
We will attract what we are.
Becoming who we are supposed to be,
Is finding the courage...
To show up and be seen.
We will find our people.
Everything will align.
It is all in the courage,
That we will SHINE.

I Am Free

My hair, blowing in the wind.
Messy.
Tangles.
I am free.
This wind.
This breeze.
Blowing through my hair.
This is bliss.
I am free.
I am falling.
Falling into space.
Space for me.
I am free.
This air.
This warmth.
The sunlight on my skin.
The clouds,
That soar right above me.
I feel this bliss.
This bliss in the air.
My feet in the grass.
My feet in the dirt.
My feet on this earth.
The earth is free.
My toes dig in.
The ground is so soft.
I fall back and land.
I lay in the grass.
My arms are free.
I lay on the ground.

Taking in the earth energy.
I fill up.
I am fulfilled.
I am grounded.
I am free.
This body of water.
This water is healing.
The water flows,
It just keeps flowing.
The water and the wind,
Create these waves.
Some waves are high.
Some waves are low.
Some come crashing down.
Some are soft.
These waves,
They flow.
They just keep flowing.
The trees,
They sway.
The leaves,
They fall.
The trees are sturdy.
The branches are free.
The roots beneath me.
They spread.
The roots keep the tree grounded.
I am like this tree.
When my feet meet the earth,
That's when I feel sturdy.
That's when I feel safe.
That is all that I need.

Sunlight.
Clouds.
The sky and the water.
The ground of the earth.
The dirt between my toes.
The grass that holds my body,
As I lay here in nature.
Nature is my boost.
Nature is bliss.
Nature is where I feel so connected.
Connected to freedom.
I am free.

Thank you.
Sending you strength.

Each and every person who has had a space in my life,
I love you dearly and thank you for making space in
your life and your heart for me.
Thank you to the people who have taken the time to
understand me & given me endless support.
I appreciate you all so much.

& To my readers,
Thank you for reading the words I write.
Learning to love yourself is a rewarding journey,
filled with hardships, pain, and realizations.
I admire and support you as you move
through your journey.

I dedicate this book to Beemer.
Thank you for teaching me unconditional love.

Printed in the USA
CPSIA information can be obtained
at www.ICGtesting.com
CBHW070621201124
17649CB00039B/745

She lost herself.
Herself, as she knew her.
She lost herself.
The self she had built.
She lost herself,
Or so she thought.
This was actually the path,
To find her true self.
She had to lose herself,
In order to find.
In order to find her true, authentic self.
She lost herself,
The self that she was.

ISBN 979-8-9912545-0-2